THERE WAS NO LINKIN' TO WHAT I WAS THINKIN'

Stan Johnson

iUniverse, Inc.
New York Bloomington

There Was No Linkin' To What I Was Thinkin'

iUniverse books may be ordered through booksellers or by contacting:

iUniverse
1663 Liberty Drive
Bloomington, IN 47403
www.iuniverse.com
1-800-Authors (1-800-288-4677)

ISBN: 978-1-4401-1363-5 (sc)
ISBN: 978-1-4401-1364-2 (ebk)

Printed in the United States of America

iUniverse rev. date: 02/11/2009

INTRODUCTION

January 23, 2002 at the age of forty-two the doctor walked back
into the exam room with the diagnosis—Parkinson's disease.
Everyone associates tremors with this disease, but one of the
lesser known symptoms is in some people their sleep patterns
are disrupted. After watching the 658th infomercial on TV I
wondered if there wasn't something else that I could do with
this time of peace and quiet that is at two in the morning. The
idea of being productive was seconded by my lovely bride of
twenty-five years, her thoughts being, folding clothes, dishes,
etc. That was the motivation for doing something else, but
writing? I honestly do not know where that idea came from
(after you read the book you may wonder the same thing). The
numerous items that I wrote throughout the years of going to
school were not met with good grades or encouraging remarks.
I did not set out to write a book, I just wrote a few stories for
my own amusement…what else was there to do? I shared a
few with fellow church members and fellow educators, and

they are the ones to blame…they gave me positive feedback, so I wrote more.

I'm convinced that I had ADD as a child. I could not sit and read through a book. I could read short stories. That problem has carried on over into my writing. The title describes how the stories contained in this book are arranged. The stories are not linked to each other, totally random. It is not something that lends itself to reading several chapters at a time. As you read I must warn you that often the beginning of a story is not a direct link to the ending, random is a good word. If these stories had a design or purpose it would be one of the following; the readers goes…hum…hadn't thought of that or maybe you will remember a time past and smile, finally I pray that you will be encouraged, and your load lightened on your journey home.

Table of Contents

Chapter 1
APRIL 27, 1975

One of the things I like to do is access old newspapers from significant years of my life, say the year I turned sixteen, and look at the ads. It is fun to see what cars sold for new, the style of clothes that people wore, the price of gas, to name a few of the items that change drastically over time. Now with the internet you can go to one of many websites that will tell you what happened on a particular day. For example, the day you were born, you can find out what was happening around the world on that special day. You may find that something fascinating or historic happened on your birthday. An infamous day in my life was April 22, 1975. My birthday? Nope. My wedding day? No that is June 20, 1980 and by the way only forgotten…twice. If you look up April 22, 1975, worldwide I don't think you will find any significance to that date. My apologies if that happens to be your birth date. That was the date that three brothers Don, Doyle, and Hershel (my dad), who all are supposedly of sound mind, did indeed follow through on the idea to start a joint business venture. They did so without consulting the *workforce* of this venture; Manuel, Archie, Joey, Mark and me, all of whom are children of the three entrepreneurs. That was the day I came home to find out that we were the owners of… Cows. Let me say it again…Cows! Not just a few cows with cute little names such as Daisy, or Gertrude, although throughout the next four years, three months and seven days many of the cows would be given unkind names which generally were given them in the heat of some confrontation. Not just a few, this was a HERD….of cows! The *workforce* would have opted for a hunting and fishing guide service or producing sports videos, but we were not consulted! We got cows! This herd was not composed of registered cows from some exotic breed, there were all kinds black, white, red, black and white, red and white, no horns, and two horns. One cow even had a single horn; the other horn being a casualty of aggression. From that display of aggression, she was told that she was going to be turned into pork chops. Pork chops…well in Don's defense, it is hard to think in a state of panic.

I'm sure during that time span there were afternoons and Saturdays that we did other things. I'm sure there was? What I remember is feeding, hauling hay, fixing fence, chasing cows, fixing fence. And if you have never seen the miracle of the live birth of a cute little calf being brought into this world and are considering searching out the opportunity to do such…. DON'T! You will be scarred for life. Then there is that bull to steer procedure. Periodically the whole herd would be gathered into a corral, and run single file down a chute into a head gate. The head gate secured the cow between the head and shoulders allowing the *workforce* the opportunity to treat the cows while they are immobile. Some of the procedures were unpleasant for the cow, but necessary. One time a cow that I will call Jezebel due to her lack of any redeeming qualities, was the last one in the corral. On this particular day I don't know if she remembered previous encounters, heard the commotion or what, but Old Jez made a decision that she was leaving and not coming back. Over the gate, down the hill, over the fence and out of sight… gone and not coming back.

Jezebel provided some high drama and adventures over the next two weeks. The day after her decision to leave she was tracked two miles away to a fenced wooded area. I still don't know what the plan was that day to recapture her. All I know was that Mark and I, the youngest of the *workforce,* were placed at the only opening with instructions not to let her out, while they went and found her. "Don't let her out" that's it? Moments later coming down the hill is a black, seventeen hundred pound cow charging full throttle. So waving a stick, yelling, and my waving arms deters this cow none, I finally realize…she's not going back. My brain was saying "hold your ground", my feet were saying "abort the mission". The feet won. I turned to Mark, who at that very instant, stick in hand, was being tossed many feet in the air. Did they think she was just going to stop and stand there while someone went and got the trailer? "Don't let her out"! I don't think that one was well thought out. Jez has now tasted the thrill of human tossing. So now, not only was she not going back, she was going to have fun doing it. Her next victim, Sonny Yates, a good neighbor, wanted to help. His parked truck blocking exit, he was standing behind truck, aborts mission!! He dived into the truck, and Jez proceeded to dent the tailgate.

Later that night, Belle the family horse, who shared the *workforce's* disgust of cows, was called into duty. My dad, trying to lasso Jez only got Belle head butted in the gut a few times… abort the mission! The next two weeks, tracking, finding, human tossing, truck denting, escaping, tracking…she was not going back.

To this day Jez remains a mystery to me. What was she thinking? She left the safety of the farm, the safety of the herd, and the care of the *workforce*. She was well feed, her medical needs were attended to, and she was well taken care of. Why fend off all those people who were trying to help? Why choose a life in the wild full of a variety of dangers? The good life for what?

Look around, look in the mirror, there it is, the same reasoning, the same actions as Jez. A teenager leaves the world of sobriety for alcohol or drugs, hurting, head butting, tossing aside those who care, those who love. Are there not husbands, wives, daddies, and mommies that are doing the same thing?

Often for little or no reason leaving behind children, mate, a church for what? A mystery why people choose a life in the wild with all the injuries, and dangers over a life… a life where you are protected, cared for, and receive true love, a life in Gods pasture if you will.

The Lord is my shepherd, I shall not want.
He maketh me lie down in green pastures:
He leadeth me beside still waters.
He restoreth my soul: He leadeth me in the paths of righteousness
for his namesake.
Yea, though I walk through the valley of shadow of death, I will
fear no evil: for thou art with me
Thy rod and thy staff they comfort me.
Thou preparest a table before me in the presence of mine enemies:
Thou annoinest my head with oil: my cup runneth over
Surely goodness and mercy shall follow me all the days of my life:
And I will follow him all the days of my life

A mystery why you would run away from that!

Chapter 2
CONTENTS UNKNOWN

It could have been gold, or millions of dollars, or um let's see…rare coins. Well, the house was built in the nineteen twenties when people just didn't trust banks. People who had treasures did not store them in banks; they stashed them away in secret places in and around their houses. The house was home for me until my junior year in high school. *I know what else it could have been; top secret documents hidden there by the CIA, yea I bet that's it.* This house was made a wonderful home by the people who lived in it, not the house itself. This big two story house must have been a house built by a well to do family because it would have been one of the finest in its day. By the standards for today's homes let me say, well it was lacking in several areas. *No, it wasn't* CIA *papers; it was a stash of stolen lute from a bank heist of Bonnie and Clyde.* Not lacking to the point that snow would blow in on you at night or anything like that, Grandpa Henson told me about those days. Little side note here; have you ever met anyone from that era that lived closer than two miles from the school and didn't have to walk to school? This house had stairs to the second story that went up about twelve steps then a landing area, they then turned and went up and back the opposite direction. Up twelve steps, turn to your left until your facing the opposite direction, then twelve more to the door of the second story. Making use of all the space the builders of this house had made a closet beneath the second set of stairs. If you can picture this closet, it was narrow, tall in the front, then sloping down towards the back to a very short space. The closet had clothes hanging from front to back of the closet and the clothes hung closer to the floor as you went toward the back. I don't know all the reasons the clothes were hung under the stairs, but I know that were never worn again. Come to think of it, some of those clothes were from the previous owner. This arrangement of clothes caused the very back of the closet to be pitch dark; there was no electricity. Only that one closet had no power...the rest of the house had electricity, indoor plumbing and running water. There it was...in the thick darkness at the very back of the closet in the most cramped spot imaginable was a storage chest. The chest had a rounded top, handles on each side, wide four inch bands that went around the chest. The one thing that I remember the most is the ornate hasp that secured the lid to the chest, which would have been very difficult to break into.... Had there been a lock on it! Would you like to know what was really in the chest… yea…? ME TOO! That's right, lived there fourteen years and never opened the chest to see what was in it. Why? Fear! I think about it being gold, coins, or Bonnie and Clyde's stash now. But when you are eight and afraid of your shadow that is not what you believe to be in the chest. What an eight year old knows is in the box is the dismembered remains of some unfortunate person, or even worse it housed the hideous monster that roams the house at night looking for a hand or foot to be out from under the covers. Fear kept the chest closed in the beginning, but after time the circumstances caused me to forget that it was even there. The closet being out of the way, the clothes blocking the view, and no light, all contributed to the chest being forgotten. I will never know what riches or opportunities were held in that unlocked chest.

This causes me to wonder, not about what was in the chest but dreams, opportunities, and even responsibilities that you and I may have or had at one time. Is fear keeping you from following a dream that you have? Is fear keeping you from a responsibility? Are those fears as unrealistic as mine were at age eight? Maybe time, and events of life are like the clothes; blocking your view to the dream or opportunity that you have. Most fears are unfounded products of a persons worrying imagination. Don't let fear keep you from following a dream. Maybe you need to get a light and shine it on your dream to bring it back to life, or, shine the light on that something or someone that needs you to overcome fear and fulfill a responsibility.

I wonder what Jesus meant when he said "seek and you will find"? God rains down blessing after blessing even at times when we don't bother to ask. Could that word *seek* mean that at times to receive a blessing from God we may have to go looking for it. *Seek*, is that something done casually or is there purpose involved? Does it mean that at times we are going to have to push through whatever has been blocking the way, get a light, and overcome some fear to open the chest to receive promises, blessing from God. I wonder!

We are also told that there is a mansion being built for us by some well-to-do individuals and we should be storing our treasures there. It's easy sometimes to let the events of life become like clothes blocking the view of the treasure. Sometimes the influence of the world creeps in and from a lack of courage causes us to lose sight of the chest of treasures. We are told to have no fear; HE is with us. You know if I would have asked, my Dad he would have gone with me and we could have opened that chest together. This is the treasure no one wants to miss out on. Have courage, don't let life block your view; get on your knees and one day the chest will be opened to you.

When we moved, no one thought to look in that out of the way closet. The next tenants inherited some very useless old clothes. You know I bet that chest is still there! I think I'll ask the people who live there if I can go look. No, on second thought I've just now gotten to where I can stick a foot or hand outside the covers. Wouldn't want to turn that monster loose!

Chapter 3
TEARS IN YOUR EARS

It's the four year anniversary of one of those days. Do you remember where you were, what you were doing, when the news of President Kennedy's death reached you? Or September 11, 2001? Every detail remains vivid in your memory. Not just what you were doing, where you were, who was with you, but you also remember the feelings, the emotions that swarmed you on that day. Kennedy's death and Sep. 11 are days that have national if not worldwide importance. What I am talking about are those days that happen in our own lives that go unnoticed to the rest of the world but to us personally, they are just as significant as a national crisis Bet you can remember every detail about your day, who you were with, where you were, how you felt, your reaction. That day that put you on your back to where *tears are running back into your ears*. As I write this it is late at night, the house is silent, Kenna is asleep and I have time to reflect on that day four years ago when I lay on my back with *tears running back into my ears.*

We are an independent bunch we are. We display to others what we have and who we want others to think we are. We may not say it but often our attitude of "Look at what I have done", "Look at what I have" shines through. We do things our way and with little help from others. Well, "I was the one who got the master's degree", "I am the one that worked hard and moved up the ladder at the company". "No one else in my family had gone this far." We hold our head up high and are as proud as we can be. In doing all this we begin to focus out in front of us and around us. We focus way down the road. Goals seem important to us and other things begin to dominate our lives. We constantly look at what is coming over the horizon. That's what we drive toward, that becomes our focus.

We begin to listen to others as to what is important. They tell us that things are important, Money is important. The more you have the happier you will be. With television, radio, and magazines, we are surrounded by voices telling us what we need and who we have to be to be happy. Telling us the direction we should set our compass.

Then you have one of those days, the phone call, the x-ray, the test result, the desperate situation, the crisis that puts you on you on your back with tears running back into your ears. At the time all may seem hopeless, but if you are indeed flat of your back with tears in your ears you are now in a position that God can use you, a position of personal growth, and help to others. You see, when you are on your back, the things that were around you that seemed so important, the things that you searched for on the horizon, they go out of focus. You can't see them because you are now looking and focused on the direction, heavenward, that we all should have been all along. I realize that God made me, he sustains, and he is in control. He has promised, and it was no pinkie promise, that if I love him it all works out for good.

When those tears have filled your ears it tends to block out all the clutter the world convinced you was important and now you listen. As you listen to the sound of your heart beat and nothing else, that is when we are more capable of talking to and listen to God.

I am not suggesting that God causes these things to happen. Nor am I suggesting that when bad things happen that it is punishment for some wrong. Bad things happen to good people. I try not to ask why, because often there is no answer. But when you get in that position and you are focused the direction you need to be looking and tuned into the correct source, God can use you. So when the crisis passes, and you no longer have tears running into your ears, keep your focus upward and listen.

Chapter 4
THE WILDERNESS TRIP
(LIFE!)

Oh, I'm not sure this is a good idea. The thought occurs to me as our only connection to the real world, picked up enough speed to lift off the water, bank to the left, and disappeared over the trees. For two years now, this trip had been on our minds daily. All the birthday and Christmas gifts were geared for this day...e-mails back and forth, excitement, abundant anticipation, and the personal packing list. The plan: Simple... be flown into the Canadian wilderness then paddle our way out for nine days. But now, I'm not sure we should have let that plane go. Now it is just us nine men, canoes packed with what we are trusting is everything we will need for nine days in the wilderness. The outfitter told us it was all we needed. Food, cooking items, tents, sleeping bags, all in five large packs. The assurance of the outfitter I begin to doubt, because of the nine men, three are still growing boys at ages 18, 19, and 20. Eating was one big question. I have seen these three in action and you can't pack enough food in four canoes to feed those three for nine days.

"Mike, could you repeat what you just said one more time. Okay that is not funny, ha ha, you got me. What! You're not kidding! Start a signal fire, flares, whatever, get that pilot's attention to turn around. ONE pack is NOT enough food"!

Then there is the briefly afore mentioned personal items list that Mike said we could bring. I mentioned it only briefly because there was so little to it. We were told to travel as lightly as possible. Some of the minor things were to cut most of the handle off your toothbrush, take the cardboard center out of your toilet tissue, as well as other small things. Then the big stuff, the important stuff; my reaction... where is the rest of the list! This is not acceptable, three changes of clothes! Shoes, pants, shirts, and maybe socks I could get by on, but three pair of underwear...no way. And get this; the three pair included the ones I had on! You do the math, three pair for nine days. We did all we could to save space, even the unreasonable. Then just at the last moment, then just then Cliff breaks out his fishing tackle box. It is a Samsonite, jumbo suitcase. It was huge. We all could have packed nine more pair of underwear into that thing.

Plane gone, canoes loaded, including the ONE food pack, doubt rising. So we pair off and get in our canoes. First, a little background on the basics of canoeing. A canoe is somewhat like a see saw, the back goes down the front goes up and visa versa. What is ideal is if the canoe is level. Okay now picture this me (300 pounds) in the front, Cliff (180 pounds) in the back. Our canoe looked like it was doing a nose dive into the water. I turn around and Cliff can't touch the water with his paddle. Where's that plane? We have to put more weight on Cliff's end. The tent pack and Cliff's tackle box did the trick. Because of the weight in our canoe, Cliff and I saw a different trip than everyone else. Ours was always from behind. Even me getting up early and loading our stuff into one of the "faster" canoes did not help.

The experience and events of those nine days are as fresh today in my memories as the day they happened. Looking back I can see many everyday life lessons that apply to the Christian who is also on a journey. I share some of those with you.

The outfitter gave us a set of maps with our route from lake to lake to our final destination marked. As a side trip he marked a place where there were Indian rock paintings called petrographies. We discussed if we wanted to take the detour. It was decided that we wanted to go. I was not part of the "we" that wanted to go. This little jaunt took two hours of paddling into the wind, both ways! I bet that outfitter is really getting a good laugh because the rock painting turned out to be one red handprint and one orange circle that I assumed was the sun. Two hours, into the wind...both ways. But you know the devil does that to us. He entices us to detour off our path. On the surface it sounds good, sounds fun, exciting. If we ever bite and start down his path it is never what you thought it was going to be, and it will be a struggle there and back. The Lords brother, James, tells us that if we resist the devil he will flee from us. "We" did manage to take 17 pictures of the two drawings.

We would be traveling down one lake and the wind would be blowing directly into our faces, which made the going more difficult. We would think that when we turn the next corner the wind will be at our back, wrong! Nine days we paddled, seventy two miles and I promise that seventy one and three tenths of those miles were paddled into the wind. In your life has the wind always been at your back? I bet there have been times when you had struggles of various kinds in your life. Like the wind in your face making things tougher. Keep paddling, bend your back and keep paddling. Though the going may at time be hard you are getting closer to your destination. Keep paddling!

Mike was our leader. He planned the entire trip down to a tee and that is not a t-shirt, we weren't allowed those. He had been on this trip two previous times, so he knew what we needed (I would still argue the three underwear thing). He told us what to expect on the trip and what to watch out for. When they started to hang the food in the trees the first night, I was let in on another secret, there are BEARS! So the one pack has to feed those three boys and possibly bears. Can we get that plane back in here? Mike had the map and knew the way to go. I will admit there were times that I knew that he was taking us the wrong way only for it to be the right way. Although, I didn't find a lot of humor when on day four after breakfast Mike says "has anyone seen the maps? I can't find them". You know, we have a savior who to our benefit and assurance has been on this trip before. He tells us exactly what we need for the trip. He tells us what to expect and he leads us the direction to go. There are times that we doubt and wonder if where he is leading us is the right way. Have faith and follow him. What reassurance to know that he has already been on this trip and he is taking care of us.

On the way to Canada, I bought a book that I was going to read; I carried it with me the whole trip, and never opened it. I carried a spare fishing reel, but never took it out of the case. Cliff's stash of fishing gear was hardly used at all. These were all examples of things we though we had to have, things we thought we really needed. Things that, in reality, only added weight and had to be carried overland from one lake to the next one. They actually slowed us down. We all do that in life. We carry stuff that we just can't let go of on our Christian journey. Things that add a burden slow us down. On this (life) trip it's okay to litter. We don't know what each is carrying, but search your life, throw them down, cast them off and leave them behind. We even had enough food for the trip. Freeze dried doesn't take up much room.

No one was in a canoe by themselves; there was at least two in each. When it was time to carry canoes, packs, paddles, all the gear over land, we all helped each other. When Dan and Jeff thought they would go through the rapids instead of around by land, we all helped fish them and their gear out of the water. They were not carrying the ONE pack of food!

There are many real threats and mishaps that could occur in that wilderness that it would be much more difficult for one person to survive alone. We need each other. There are mishaps, there are rapids to go around, stuff to carry that we all in real sense need each other to make it to our destination.

The adventure, scenery, camaraderie, eagles, the abundance of fish, the moose, all which went into this trip, changed my attitude through the nine days. It was beautiful, fun, exciting, and scary at times. It was exhausting. It was a learning experience; I now know how to wash and manage three changes of clothes for nine days and have clean underwear every day. In a word, it was wonderful, so wonderful that day nine got there too fast. It was over long before I wanted it to be. And day seven, eight, and nine were the fastest. Life is great, wonderful, scary, exciting all those things. But most of all it is brief. Again James tells us we are but like a vapor that rapidly disappears. Don't waste a second. Ah shucks, here comes the plane.

The trip was great as I stated. It was like nothing I had experienced before. And I plan on going back someday to visit again. But I found something else out on that trip. The wilderness was a great place to visit but I don't belong there permanently. Once the trip was over and throughout the trip I was wishing for home. As great as the trip was, I still remember the reception from my wife and daughters when we got home.

I remember the feeling of being home. This life is a journey, it's all the things I have already stated, but it's not home. We are not made to stay in the wilderness. Home is better. It is beyond what we can humanly imagine.

If you ever go on a trip like this, give me a call. I can tell you nine places to hide clean underwear. Sorry Mike, there are limits to what I'll sacrifice.

Chapter 5
I GOT ONE---Ouch!

Some of them are fast as lightning when they are discovered. There they are then you blink and they are gone. Then there are those that don't move so fast because they don't realize that they have been uncovered. Once they figure it out whoosh they are gone. Finally the ones that know they are seen and don't care, those are the ones that have a nasty disposition. They sit there with their modified arms in the air daring anything to come close. Any of the three will attempt to inflict pain if captured. Crawdads, not just fishing bait but a source of fun for our family. It is amazing how kids can take simple things; sticks, a ball, pine cones, dirt, or any other simple object and a little imagination and build anything, and entertain themselves for hours. X-Box, Nintendo, IPods, who needs them when you have a nearby stream that is chock full of crawdads. One of our favorite things to do in the summer was to take a green pickle bucket, and go to Bennett's Creek, which was ideal for little kids to play. Fresh clean water flowing slowly and shallow enough to be safe for kids, and it had crawdads, lots of them, one under every stone. Two adults, three kids, green pickle bucket, and Nubbin (the pet miniature dachshund) would load into a 1978 Chevy Caprice. This car was once the family car that we drove to work or church. Due to the lack of a second vehicle and my hobbies now it was the scuba diving, hunting, fishing, camping, and family car with gear and remnants from trips of all those activities still in the car, and we still drove it to work and church. For a couple of hours we would wade up and down the creek turning over rocks, catching the little fellas, and putting them in the green pickle bucket. At the end we would count how many we had caught, always trying to catch more than the time before, then we would take the crawdads and… are you ready for this…have you ever tasted fresh crawdads out of a flowing stream? We haven't either, we turned them loose. Did we know how to have fun or what!

Crawdads can be hard to catch. You turn over the rock and they are facing forward…as you reach down the critters take off backwards. Something I did not know about Kenna before I married her; she is an expert crawdad catcher, the best I had ever seen. Had her Dad known this he may have gotten seven more years of labor out of me. We had made two or three trips and Courtney, age two, (I said it was safe and slow flowing) had not caught one, but it was not because she had not been persistent. I was close to her that day when finally as excited as she had ever been yelled "I got one, I got one." All is not well though, for the Ipod generation let me explain the important feature of a crawdad, they have two overgrown pinchers for defense. Her face now grimacing, she repeats the announcement while taking the crawdad into the other hand. She had worked hard and was proud and she is not letting it go, never mind the pain. It was the same determination she exhibited when she decided she was not going to eat her green peas. I had been determined she was going to eat them. Crawdad…you are going to lose. Pain overcoming pride caused her to let the crawdad go, in the bucket, but now the crawdad had her and she couldn't let go. Tears…Time…try again.

Bad habits, temptations, doing wrong, always hidden waiting to be uncovered and picked up. It is not the fact that we all have to deal with the temptation and fall into these that is important but <u>how</u> we deal with them that is what is important. How many times do we go hunting for these things thinking that we can handle them safely and we won't get pinched, without pain? We catch them thinking that we are in control and can turn them loose when in fact they have us and we can't turn them loose. Some are slow; some are fast as lightning. We should never go hunting for bad habits, temptations, wrongs; we should leave them under the rocks where they belong. When you find one, don't pick it up thinking you can turn it loose. They will inflict pain.

Kenna was already good at catching the critters, and the kids honed their skill over time. You gotta be quick and brave; well, I held the bucket and counted.

Chapter 6
WHAT KINDA
HOUSE YOU HAVE

They have all kinds of names; Tudor, Ranch, Victorian. What kind of house do you have? Take highway 101 north out of Gamaliel, Arkansas until you get to county road 125, turn left, and follow that road until you see a cattle gate on your right. You are now on private property known as the Old Beene Farm. Follow the dirt path for about two miles and there it was. Sitting near a spring-fed creek was the most wonderful log cabin I have seen to date. It had everything a person could want, it lacked nothing. Whoever built this house knew what they were doing. This log house did not come from one of those magazines where you buy the kit and snap it together model of the twenty first century. This home was built from logs that were individually cut, by hand, and shaped to fit tightly with each other. The roof had wooden slates that were hand made. All this without the use of power tools. This house was built in the mid 1800's. The detached restrooms are no longer standing, a sign of lesser workmanship or the victim of being turned over too many times. This house is functional, serving the needs of the occupants.

The builder was one of frugality. The logs are rough; run your hand over these you will get splinters. The owners had not wasted anything even making use of the burlap sacks the flour had come in to serve as a window covering. Not as curtains but as the barrier between the inside and the outside. A peek inside and you see the interior decorator had been working, at one time having tacked numerous cardboard boxes flat to the wall to cover cracks. The running water came running out of the well…if you pumped the handle fast enough. Neither was the house cluttered with all that electrical stuff that takes up space and eats up energy of today's homes. Heat and air…definitely, there was heat in the summer and cold in the winter. What kind of house do you have?

Wonderful? Lacking nothing? Everything you need? I sense you doubting the glory of this house. But you did not see what I saw that October afternoon when my Mom took us back to her childhood home. You did not see the tears of happiness as she walked the premises, with the aid of a walking stick, event after event of her early childhood past rushed back into her adult present. I heard the tone of her voice after each story came back to her as she passed them on to her children and grandchildren. A boulder in back was place where it was made to look like "Santa" had dropped her candy one Christmas morning, complete with deer tracks. No, this home lacked nothing a child needed, and would be the envy of many a person living in some houses with electricity and running water. Don't get the wrong picture, times were very difficult for the Henson family, but that house was occupied by a mother and father who were devoted to and committed to each other well beyond fifty years; a bond broken only by the passing of my grandfather at the age of 93. The house was about the care and well-being of the children. What did this house have that made it special? Love, not the sensual "love" portrayed on TV, nor the, I can't sleep for thinking about you love. This love was a love of sacrifice; thinking about the other person, putting them first. The kind of love that Christ has for each of us. How do I know this when this house, now abandoned, was occupied long before I was born? I saw those qualities lived out everyday in my mother. She had her faults, though as time goes by, I don't remember them as well. The most outstanding quality was her love for her family. I don't know the name of the type of house that I grew up in, but I know how the home was built and that was on the sacrificial love of Mom. What kind of house do you have?

Steele, Missouri off T highway was another house that sat on the bank of drainage ditch, Sunrise was the place. I never saw the house but I have heard the stories of snakes in the ditch, and catching carp in flooded fields. I've seen the joy in her eyes as she shared with her three children the memories of growing up. You see, the little girl that grew up in that house came to CRA her eighth grade year. When she walked by. I told my best friend that I was going to marry her one day. I was in ninth grade! I know a stupid statement at that age, but Tuesday we will celebrate our twenty-fifth anniversary. She has her faults…she says so anyway. I haven't seen them yet. But what I have seen is our family being built and sustained by that same sacrificial love.

Chapter 7
WHAT DID HE WITNESS?

I know him well; I served as second in command in four, no, it has been five locations around the world with him. We had seen a lot over the past twenty two years, but we were not prepared for *what we were about to witness.* It was Thursday evening and he had just sat down after his evening meal H*e did not know what he was about to witness.* He began to think about his family back home in Rome and he thought; "just thirty six more days and my men and I will be at the coliseum for the tour of duty that all soldiers wait for", He relaxed into a doze. H*e did not realize what he was about to witness.* Protecting the Roman interests had taken him around the world, and now Jerusalem. It had been okay, and the Jews, for the most part, were peaceful, though he could sense the hatred they had for the army that occupied their homeland. Pilate had been good to work for; they had even become friends having been invited to partake occasionally in a meal with the governor at the palace. Tomorrow he was going sleep late, and go down to the market. With the Jewish holiday of Passover coming Saturday there would need to be extra soldiers present, though not on duty, he was the kind of soldier that did what needed to be done whether it was his job or not, *he did not realize what he was going to witness.* He did not plan to attend the execution of the two thieves who had exhausted all their appeals. He had not been able to get completely past the cruelty of that form of punishment. He could remember the eight that he had been in charge of down to the tiniest detail; it would be a relief if he never saw another one.

Ordered by Pilate to find him and summon him to the governor's mansion, it takes me beating on the door a second time to awaken him. It seems that the whole town of Jerusalem and some Jews from other cities are in an uproar like none that Pilate had ever seen before, and he wanted his most trusted, most discerning soldier present. He gets to the palace before the mob shows up and finds out that the leaders of the Jews are putting Jesus on trial in their religious courts and would soon be petitioning Pilate. *He does not know what he is about to witness.* Although he did not know Jesus personally he had seen him periodically in town and had even stopped to listen to some of Jesus' oration. Being a centurion, he had investigated the stranger and found him to be no threat to the Roman government. That was his only interest in Jesus. Still, he was aware of the high emotions that Jesus had stirred in area. He had witnessed the reception that he had received just the other day, but it was a reception one would expect should Caesar come to town, and now they have him on trial in their religious council? He agrees with Pilate that this is the greatest unrest he has seen in Jerusalem. He spends his time shuttling between the gatherings of the council and updating Pilate at the governor's palace. About the time the rooster is signaling daybreak, he sends word that they are bringing Jesus to Pilate to be sentenced to death. He is ordered by Pilate to be the Centurion in command; *he does not know what he is about to witness.* I was beside him as the mob came into the courtyard, lead by Caiaphas, and handed Jesus over to him with the demand that he be...crucified.

Pilate was now prepared to see Jesus. He is standing guard listening to Pilate question Jesus, when out of the corner of his eye he sees Pilate's wife waving for him to come there. She seems to be stressed and frantically in a hurry. He returns with a warning for Pilate from his wife that Pilate should have nothing to do with this innocent man, based upon the great suffering she had endured from a dream during that night. He is witness to the interrogation of Pilate and the astounding silence of Jesus. He agreed with Pilate that the only reason they had brought him to be executed was out of their hypocrisy bring exposed. But it appears to Pilate that the only solution to keep peace and protect his authority is to kill Jesus. He now leads Jesus to be flogged, he himself not doing the flogging but still under his watchful eye. Many criminals died from this beating alone, he wishing this to be the case. Should Jesus die from the beating, the agony and the cruelty of being crucified could be avoided. The mob would be satisfied and disperse allowing him to go about his planned activities for the day. *HE DOES NOT KNOW WHAT HE IS ABOUT TO WITNESS.* The company of soldiers has to have their fun at the expense of Jesus. When he was younger he would have participated in the revelry but this time he chose not to.

He led the procession through the city and out to the "skull". The plan had been formulated. Each of the thieves would go one each side, then Jesus would go last and be placed in the middle as a kind of centerpiece. The plan goes off without a hitch, until about 3 p.m. Jesus cries with a loud voice and dies. Earthquakes, rocks split, dead people coming out of their tombs, darkness in the middle of the day. We all were terrified and that's when I heard him say about Jesus, "Surely this was the Son of God". He had witnessed the greatest event in the history of mankind. To be followed by an equally great event a few days later.

What caused him to proclaim Jesus the Son of God? The Bible says "when he saw these things"… what things. Well… darkness in the middle of the day, dead people walking around, and earthquakes. But is that all he would have seen? I think there are other possibilities that had an effect on this him. As a Roman soldier he was not able to ignore turmoil that Jesus was causing in the area. Investigating Jesus, he saw the compassion he had for the people especially children, the poor, and sick. He could tell Jesus was against pretended righteousness. His teachings were analyzed to the threat it would have to Roman rule. At least one other centurion in another city had seen and heard Jesus and believed. I believe there is more. He witnessed the compassion he had on his persecutors, on those that mocked him, on his executioners. He did not curse them like all the others; he did not hurl insults back at them. It was almost as if Jesus knew something, a secret, and felt sorry for... them. He was sure he heard Jesus say; "Father, forgive them, they don't know what they are doing". Then there was that thief who saw something in Jesus. He changed from hardened criminal to supporter. He heard Jesus telling the thief about paradise. Then when he was securing the thieves to their cross it took a band of soldiers to hold each down as the nails were driven, one almost escaping. Jesus he…he walked over to the cross unattended, lay down on the cross, stretched out his hands and waited. It was like he knew something; it was as though Jesus was doing this with purpose. It wasn't as though he was taking the life away from Jesus, it seemed like Jesus was giving it! *He knows now what he witnessed!* The Son of God crucified.

He does not have a name in the Bible. He was as close to the event that redeemed man as one could get. He witnessed all those things. He was face to face with Jesus while Jesus died for me. He is a lesson for us. What affect did this have on the rest of his life? Did the terror pass and he return to his old ways? Did he become a disciple and live the rest of his life for Jesus?

Did he change his allegiance? We don't know but we do know we are faced with Jesus we have a choice to make. Am I going to allow Jesus to control my life? *We know what he witnessed!*

Chapter 8
SOUNDS OF LOVE

Creak, crack, creak, crack of the wood floor as grandma rocks one of her loved ones to sleep. The sporadic rat tats tat of the manual typewriter where Dad was working. I've never seen anyone type so fast with two fingers. Mom humming all those tunes as she went about her chores. Sounds of love are what they are.

We experience our world through our five senses. When asked which sense they would least like to do without most people state sight. The fact is that people who lose their sense of hearing have a harder time adjusting to their surroundings. I don't know the psychological reasons for this fact. I know that much of the love we have for each other is conveyed through sound. Could it be in part the importance of hearing those sounds of love?

Sounds of love, those sounds that at the time are not in the foreground of our awareness. They are not what you are tuned into at the time. The thud of the baseball into the glove was not what you were focused on, it was the call of "strike" that you were tuned into in this make believe game with Dad. They are like the background music of a well scored movie. Seemingly insignificant at the time, but now you think back and those sounds ring loud, above whatever noise clutters your conscience. Sounds that possibly take you to another place and time. Love sounds, can you hear them? A smile spreads across your lips, feeling of contentment takes over, maybe a tear, there is peace, there is…. Well there is love as you listen to those sounds in the present or coming back to you from the past. Bacon sizzling at 6:00 in the morning by mother who made sure her kids ate breakfast before she went to work as a cook at the local school. The sound of a wife's fingers going through your hair which at one time was irritating but now helps put you to sleep. The words "If you wanna be a wheel you gotta get up and roll" being sung to you to wake you up each morning. Didn't seem like love at the time while trying to sleep…it would be love now to be able to hear it. Sounds of love, loud and clear.

The sounds were heard on these days but they were drowned out by the other activities of the day. They certainly weren't recognized as love sounds. The sound of wood sliding in the dry dirt. The sound of the groundskeeper's shovel as it slices through the sod. The echo of a hammer pounding. The sweeping sound of a broom sweeping out the building waste of a new room. Gravel being ground under the weight of a heavier object. They were there those days, screaming "I LOVE YOU" but they were not heard. They were not the focus of the people that day. They didn't recognize the sound of the cross being drug through the dirt as a "love sound". The sound of the hole being dug to support the cross, then the sound of the soldier pounding the spikes, first through flesh then wood. The new tomb being swept out for its new occupant. All saying "I loved you so much that I sent my only son that whoever believes on me will not die but live forever" Then the guards look at each other as the sound of the stone begins to grind over the smaller stones as it is rolling away from the entrance to the tomb. All love sounds we can all now hear and when we do there is comfort, there is peace, there is contentment, there is….. Well… there is love!

Chapter 9
CHURCH MEMORIES OF A FOURTEEN YEAR OLD

"Stanley Eugene Johnson come up here and set by your mother!" She just pulled out the trinity of the naming system, first, middle, and last names, which is never; let me say again, never good. Add to the fact that those words were spoken to me, by my Dad, the minister, from the pulpit, during his sermon one Sunday morning. All 299 eyes turned and looked at me, which is one hundred and fifty people, for those of you doing the math. Three lessons I learned that day, first, the amount that time slows down is directly proportional to the number of people staring at you. That was the longest walk taken to date. The second lesson came in the privacy of my parents' bedroom; age fourteen is not the age of independence. The last lesson served me well in the years to follow and that was don't believe a word that Archie and

Manuel (two cousins, two years older than me) told me. They told me that the big hair that Mrs. Waters wore every Sunday was a wig. I found out later that it would not have mattered, real hair burns also. Never trust cousins!

With seven people in the family and Dad being the minister, it was a struggle financially. Now we didn't lack for anything that we needed. As kids, we didn't get everything that we wanted. And now working in the school system with teenagers; thank you Mom and Dad for not giving me everything I wanted. Most families eat out a lot these days, mine included, but this was not the case when I was younger. Eating out at a restaurant was a treat. About the only time we ate out was when Dad preached a funeral or a wedding. As you know, it is customary to pay the preacher for these services. So there would be a little extra money we would get to go out and eat. This posed a real dilemma, and today I really feel guilty. The announcement would be made that sister or brother church member was critically ill and let's pray for their return to health. I would glance at my sister with a slight grin, a real dilemma for a fourteen year old and living in an aging community with few young couples even dating. I'm sorry, it was my only hope.

Laughing is appropriate at the right time and at age 14 I knew when one should and shouldn't laugh. And I knew this was not the time. Even armed with that knowledge and the knowledge of the consequences, it did not change the laughter attack that struck me that night. Big time preacher is holding a gospel meeting. He has just told the story about Jesus and the last supper. His topic of the lesson was the Communion. I should get points for remembering his theme, don't you think? In the preacher's emphatic voice he was going to say "fruit of the vine" instead what came out was "fruit of the loom" did anyone else catch that? The preacher didn't; he never missed a beat, kept right on going. The brain can process remarkably fast because what happened next took place instantaneously. The reaction that would occur if I did, the consequences if I did, were weighed against each other, but, I did it anyway, I looked at Archie and Manuel. No, the blunder had not escaped their keen ears. The instant eye contact was made, it wasn't the out loud burst of laughter but it was the belly laugh that shook the pew. Three boys, who despite the reverence of the setting, the looks from our parents that indicated the three of us were not long on this earth, could not make us stop laughing. Oh, there would be a brief pause, then a glance or a little snicker, then it was full pew shaking laughter all over again. Now the closing prayer and wouldn't you know it, Mr. Kincade. Loved him, everyone did, but his closing prayer was six minutes and twenty two seconds long, worded in Kings James English, blessed everything and every body, and could be recited by any member of the congregation. I waited for another lesson from the privacy of Dad's bedroom. To this day the "vine vs. loom" incident I will call it, has never been mentioned. I think I know why, because for certain I saw Mom and Aunt Ellen's pew was shaking too.

Oh, I almost forgot! I know you have been wondering. No it wasn't a misprint, 299, Mr. Jackson…hunting accident.

Chapter 10
THE STINKY FLIGHT

Having flown many times, to me, it has become routine; carry-on luggage into the overhead bin, slide into the pre-requested window seat, fasten seat belt, open magazine and wait for the remainder of the passengers to board the plane. There once was anxiety about who would be sitting in the nearby seats, now there was indifference. Not today, not with those two sitting there….

    …"Sir, you may want to come take this phone call" yelled the long-time worker to his boss who was returning from his walk down the road. Everyday, always east, looking, hoping. That was the direction the son went, two years ago, so happy and full of dreams the father let him leave. The younger of the two brothers he had not always listened to good advice. He often would have to live, to learn the hard way. This was one of those times; the father had reasoned *and warned him of the dangers of what he was about to do, and now two years no contact, no letters, no e-mails, no text message, nothing…*

The two men find their way to the last two seats empty seats on the plane. Luckily, there had been two cancellations. They had not purchased the tickets ahead and had been on standby. Neither of the two men knew that they were going to be flying today. Gasps, whispers, snickering, stares, by the other passengers as the two settle in. The smell, the filth of the younger man is appalling. For the passengers who were raised on the farm they recognize the smell of pigs, all other passengers just recognize it as stench. Why had he not cleaned up? The older gentleman is much cleaner although his clothes seem to have been soiled by the filth from the younger man. The passengers strain to listen to the conversation; big brother, the farm, Milkyway the pet cow, never eating pork again, I'm sorry, home, happiest day. Although the smell is still there, after watching these two, it goes unnoticed. It's not the grunge; what fills the air is the laughter, the joy, the tears of forgiveness, the love these two obviously have for each other. The love a father has for his son he has not seen for two years…

"Hello, this is Farside Farms." "Hello, who is speaking, please?" Softly, a voice on the other end that can barely be heard over the sound of…of pigs. "DADDY, I WANT TO COME HOME." Stop the story there, and like a movie that has alternate endings I'm going to let you choose the father's response from these options. First option; "Well son you made your bed now you are just going to have to lay in

it." How about this one; "Well son when you get home we will talk about what's next." Or does this sound better; "What is your address and I'll send you some money to get home and in all three cases be sure and clean up before you get here." Is that the picture that we have of God? Sadly, that is how we often treat sinners. If none of those suit you; me neither. I do not believe that is the way the Father is portrayed. These two men end up on the plane together because the father did whatever it took, whatever sacrifice was involved to go and get his son and bring him home. Getting his son home was it, nothing else. Let me say again, nothing else mattered. Do you think when he finally gets to his son that it mattered that his son was still dirty? Do you think the father even thought to bring clean clothes for his son? Do you think the father wanted separate seats on the plane so people wouldn't associate the two? I don't think so! Getting the son home was the one thing that mattered to the father. I doubt that either of the men noticed the reaction of the other passengers nor would they have cared. It was all about getting the son home.

The plane lands; everyone allows the two gentlemen off the plane first. For the obvious reason and the two's eagerness to get home. Having spent three hours in the presence of that father you feel blessed. You realize you have witnessed the love that God our father must have for us. Could it be that I have not messed up so much and that God will take me back? But I have gone too far from God; I have let the filth of the world cover me from head to toe. How disgusting? How far away? Not enough that God won't come and get me and take me home if he hears "Daddy I want to come home."

Chapter 11
SEE...HEAR...KNOW!

You knew it when you saw it or heard it. A snap of the fingers, a gruff "uh um", a clearing of the throat. Coach Walls, it is a shrill whistle, the kind you make with your mouth, not the kind that you blow on. For my mother, it was a certain look - pursed lips, raised eyebrows, one higher than the other, her head tilted to one side, looking over the top of her glasses. Then there was the glare of those eyes, let it be known the mom didn't give you a look, it was THE look. Not a word had to be spoken, in fact, when this dreaded episode would take place there would be deafening silence. Wow, was it effective. If you see it or hear it, you will know it. It's that unique cue that every parent has for their children. The cue that is able to bring a youngster's attention to the front and center with pinpoint focus, regardless of where that child's attention had been. As a child that cue told me *boy, you have messed up big time*, like the time I got mad in the garage and threw a wrench. My brain was racing ninety miles an hour trying to think how I was going to explain the new found hole in the freezer door. In my state of constructing a plausible story, I look at the door leading into the house and there stood Mom! She watched the whole event, silence… stillness…rigor mortis. This cue that parents have will work at close proximity, or from great distances. It does not matter, the results were the same. If you see it or hear it, the dense fog that had been clouding your judgment allowing you to do whatever you should not be doing, quickly dissipates. Suddenly you now have crystal clear thinking, complete understanding, sound reasoning, twenty/twenty vision. If you see it or hear it, all doubt is removed about your actions and there you stand, transparent, guilty, and helpless. I think I'll call Mom and confess all the things she didn't know about…Nay.

What picture would you like to have had? I often wish God would have sent Jesus to earth with today's technology. He must have sent him when he did for a reason and I am in no way questioning God. But there are pictures and videos that I would like to have. Baby pictures, wise men, the great catch of fish, and there are others but there is one in particular that is greatest interest to me. It is a picture that if we could see would have everlasting, profound effect on our lives. If you hear it or see it you will know. Peter heard it. He was warned that he was going to do it. "I don't know him"…he did not see it. "I told you I don't know him"… he still did not see it. Get the camera ready! Third time, cursing " I do not know him." The rooster crows, then Peter sees it. Mark 12:61 *And the Lord turned and looked at Peter.* Stop… Click…Did you capture that moment. What do you see? Did he turn to the left or the right? Are there still drops of blood on his face from the garden? Was it a look of loneliness, hurt, what was it? Were his eyes wet with tears? Don't miss a detail of this picture. Burn this image into your conscience. Carry it with you everywhere you go. The next time you are tempted to sin, pull this picture out and see what Peter saw. Today carry this image with you. Before you say those hurtful words…see the picture. Before you (whatever your temptation)…can you see it?

Peter saw, all doubt was removed. There he stood transparent, guilty, and helpless. He left immediately and wept bitterly. I wonder…I wonder if this look that Peter saw is repeated each and every time by Jesus. Repeated each time I sin. I doubt Peter ever forgot what he saw that day! It is my prayer that we can see it and never forget.

If you hear it or see it you will know!

Chapter 12
THE ONE SIDED PICTURES

Going through the "picture drawer" looking for pictures to use for the homecoming next month, she comes across some proofs of my senior pictures. The *picture drawer*- those two drawers that we had been taught to get out of the house first should the house catch on fire-then go back in and get the people out. She fans through the proofs and just by chance she noticed something. She said nothing but curiously looked back through the proofs carefully. Don't they take poses from both sides for senior picture? This must be a cheap photographer who was in a hurry, but a glance at the bottom of the pictures reveals the name of the best photographer around at the time. She knows her dad well and he doesn't have any scars or such on the left side of his face. She doesn't ask then but later she couldn't let it go and had to ask, "What's the deal? Why are all your senior pictures of only one side of your face?" She had to ask!

I now have to explain to my daughter that there was indeed a physical reason why the photographs were done like they were. A temporary injury caused by the action of two character traits that are present in a lot of people, especially eighteen year olds. These two traits are independent, yet they usually go hand in hand. When you have a large dose of one, the other will manifest itself in epic proportions. I speak from experience. Stupidity; known as the "s" word at our house, the trait that leaves others around you dumbfounded, not at your success or failure at what a person just said or did, but that you would even think it. I wish I could say that after eighteen it diminishes in everyone, in most, but not all. Funny thing is that despite all of life's experiences the "s" word can rear its head at any age. Well, it isn't funny if you are the one who is acting in such a way. Some actions have greater consequences than others when the "s" word is exhibited. I had a moment at eighteen, thus the one sided pictures.

When you live a couple of miles from town, own an extremely short attention span and grow up before video games anyway, you find creative things for entertainment. The safe play baseball, basketball, batting rocks, exploring, swimming in the creek (depended on who was at the swimming hole from town whether or not it was safe). Then the…well, more creative activities; dirt clod fights, tearing down wasp nest, bottle rockets at thirty paces, skinny dipping (again depended on who was

at the swimming hole), getting in Mr. Hill's cherry tree. Then
when one sibling tries to out do the other (my brother, who was
three years older, and I were just a little bit competitive, a little).
I don't know how it started but we ended up with a homemade
high jump contraption. A couple of saplings buried about two
feet into the ground sticking up as standards, some nails for
pegs to hold the crossbar, and a crossbar. A couple important
notes here: first unless you have a bunch of old mattresses to
land on you better learn to land on your feet. Second, you want
the crossbar to be lightweight and flimsy so when you miss…
"Joey when your leg quits bleeding we will throw the 2" x 4"
away and find another crossbar, flimsier."

One March afternoon my sisters and I were walking from
the barn to the house. My four older sisters, (yes older, that
makes me the youngest, and I hate being called the baby), were
already not living at home so they had not seen my expertise at
the high jump, and I was enlightening them as to what a talented
younger brother that they had become. Then she asked… I'm
not certain the question was for honest information or if it
was asked knowing it would get a response. The question, "Can
you jump that?" was bait or a dare, from an *older sister.* My
good sense should have recognized the question for what it
was, but PRIDE caused me to do something incredibly stupid.
Running…faster…closer… judge the distance…kick right leg
high,…plant left foot…wet clay, almost. Almost over… NO…
almost completely through it. I am now hanging, tangled in
a four strand barbed wire fence. That's right, in the question

"Can you jump that?" the "that" she was referring to was the fence that had barbs on it to keep the horses in the pasture. Not one, but four. Once free, my only injury was four big scratches down one side of my face. This does not include the destruction of my pride that was finished off by the continuous laughter of the witnesses. Grandchildren, your own kids, hard work, others, 23 inch trout are a few of the things that you can be proud of, but when you spend it on yourself watch out! Solomon had a few things to say about pride in Proverbs.

Proverbs 11:2 When pride comes, then comes disgrace, but with humility comes wisdom.
Proverbs 16:18 Pride goes before destruction, a haughty spirit before a fall.
Proverbs 29:23 A man's pride brings him low, but a man of lowly spirit gains honor.

Fall, lack of wisdom, destruction, low, sounds like pride can hang you upside down tangled in a fence. Thus the one sided senior pictures only because of pride mixed with the "s" word.

Experience is the great teacher. I have since learned to determine when a question is bait and I retired from high jumping…completely…anything. Although, a couple of months later I did clear the fence, sailed right over it. Had I not learned my lesson? Yes, I was smarter. It was not an exhibition of pride again, but I was holding on for dear life on the back of a spooked horse named Roxy.

Chapter 13
THE NUDGE

Questions, I only have questions. Twenty-three years ago I had all the answers, now only questions. She was only two and this was the first snow that she was going to get to play in with her big brother. School was closed so I did not have to work and was looking forward to sleeping past 5:30 when I normally got up to drive the bus. "No honey, let's wait until the sun comes up." She had raised her blinds and peeked out the window, snow! It is 6:00 and she is ready to play. I had hoped for a much later beginning to this day but my kind, gentle, soft, request (she does not remember it that away) did nothing to deter her excitement. Everyone in the house now awake assembles in the living room to make a game plan. This was one of many ploys used to occupy the minds of the two kiddos who are charged on two-twenty volts. The older brother had already escaped out the sliding back door, made a flying circle around the swing set, barefooted and in his underwear, which were always on backwards. I promise we were good parents. Watchful, we were conscientious parents, but sometimes kids, they, sometimes they just, well, they just do "stuff." We were able to delay the inevitable until the sun had come up and made the conditions outside tolerable. The plan was to find a side road with no traffic and one more very important criteria; a hill.

"No honey you can't go run around the swing barefoot in your underwear." "I know he did." Now one of the things that can't be described only experienced, getting kids ready to play in the snow, WOW. Thermals, socks, sweat pants, jeans, sweat shirt, boots, coat, wool cap with ear coverings; she's ready and I'm exhausted. The four of us, with all our winter clothes, blankets, and our all important toboggan, pile into a Volkswagen Rabbit. No car seat this time. We were so compact no one was going anywhere should we wreck. Across town to our friends' apartment who live on a dead end street with a nice long, gently sloped hill. This was a big snow by Arkansas standards; about eight inches so everything was covered and the snow had drifted to fill the road ditches.

Last minute instructions; hold on tight, don't lean over or you will fall; daddy will be right there. I'm going to give her a little push, just enough to slide her along where I can jog beside and stop her if needed. We think one trip would be enough, then let big brother ride all he wanted (who to this day is an adrenaline junkie, just not barefoot and in his underwear). A slight push…all is well, then….wait, miscalculation, the hill is steeper than I thought and the snow is slicker than I thought. Every second the faster she goes; I now realize that she is soon going to be going faster than I can run. I reach out to grab her coat; she is now beyond my reach. I keep running but the gap is getting wider. I look up and see the hazards, a tree zooms past her, watch out for that stranded car, I am frantic but worst of all I'm helpless. Courtney is looking at me laughing, having the time of her life. She thinks this is the way it was supposed to go. She is not aware of all the dangers that are swishing past her.

We had hoped to delay it as long as we could. We had used every ploy known to parenthood. But all three of them had lifted the blinds of parental protection and peeked out to see…the world, life on their own. "No, honey wait until the conditions are better." They need more time to prepare, get ready. It's not time yet! So we feed them, teach them, prepare them to go. Neither parent or child is living in reality. The parent wants to keep them inside protected; child wants to run around the swing barefoot and in his underwear. The plans are just to give them a little nudge, run along beside and grab them if needed. So we do, nudge them out into life, running after them, but as time passes the gap widens and they are more on their own. Watch out for that…, don't run into ….we often see the dangers. We make an attempt to gather them back, too late, looking on helpless. But you know what I've noticed? They are having the time of their lives going out and growing themselves. There will be crashes. So we keep running to be there when they need us. We help pick them up, dust off the snow, bandage the wounds, and GULP, nudge them back down the hill again. We watch. Questions, now only questions. Did we instill right from wrong? Were we too strict, not strict enough? Did we give them the skills to survive? Do they know that we love them unconditionally? I believe God is a better parent than we can imagine or experience here on earth. He is beside us, guiding us, but leaving us to make choices. Do we crash in life from time to time? He is at our side. He picks us up, dusts us off, treats the wound and nudges us back into life. And he wants us to miss the hazards and have the time of our lives.

Courtney, laughing, zips to the bottom of the hill, all the way to the bottom where she lands softly in a snow drift. I arrive moments later, in dire need of oxygen, ready to console her through this traumatic experience, only for her to look up and say; "Do it again daddy." I pray that their lives will be the same. Back home, take off the winter clothes, hot chocolate and cookies. Nap time but first out the door around the swing set ....kids just do stuff!

Chapter 14
DON'T DESTROY THE SNOW!

Children across this country have a universal distaste for them. Disgusting, they are! Even at a young age, a child is able to understand the implications of their terrible deed. Who's responsible? Whose invention was this, the devil himself? Rich or poor, girl or boy, city or country, public enemy number one…. SNOW PLOWS! The destroyer of dreams.

The child, oblivious to all things said and done around them, does not miss that one statement by the weather man; "There is a 20% chance of snow a week from Thursday." No doubt in their minds, the snow of the century is about to strike. And they begin to prepare; sled…check, gloves…check, boots… check, button…check, coal…check, old grey hat…check. (At least mom and dad wait until Tuesday to…you know a thought… could the baking and dairy industries be behind this prediction?) Dreams, snowball fights, snow cream, sledding until your toes feel like frozen bricks, no school until next year, and snow cream (milk). Everyone at home together, Dad and I building the world's biggest snowman and snow fort, helping Mom bake chocolate chip cookies, collecting clean snow for… Dreams.

Tuesday, sunshine but cold, and the weather channel now says 50%. The child no doubt, still preparing. Wednesday, cloudy and cold 70%. Wednesday evening, cloudy cold 70%, he can't sleep. Thursday morning cloudy cold, catch the bus for school! Then, in Mrs. Midge's reading class, we all saw…flakes. Mr. Sander's math lesson, the beep from the intercom, the Principal, total spontaneous joy. They do come true…Dreams.

As I have grown into adulthood, my distaste for snow plows has not diminished. I understand the safety issues of being able to safely navigate the highways. I understand that a healthy commerce depends on people being able to travel. But having tasted the high stress, fast paced, go faster world of adulthood, I wonder. I wonder if snow days are gifts from God. His way of giving us time; time to play, time to enjoy, rest, contemplate what and who is important, dream, fulfill dreams. His way of saying; "Stop, be still, know that I am God."

Thursday night against the moonlit snow flashes the amber light of the snow plow. It's deed now done. The highways are cleared. What was that the weather man said about Friday… DREAMS?

Chapter 15
WHAT DOES IT MEAN
TO THE PARENTS?

Three kids from the same two parents growing up in the same house, you would think that they would be similar. Actually, I expected them to be almost identical. That was before they were born. After the first two were born and the third one was on the way, reason says that she will be like one of the other two. Not so. Three children, three very different people. The only thing they share in common is that they have two legs, two arms, two eyes and so on. That is it, though. In the things that really make humans individual people they are different, very different. *What does this mean to the parents?* For starters, it does not matter what you have done to the nursery. It does not matter what experts you have read. You are not ready for what has entered your life. It does not matter how determined you are, how smart you are, or how patient you are. You will be at some time reduced to a dazed, confused, sniffling, retreating, broken shell of a human huddled in a corner. Let us visit the topic of the number of children a couple should have. Ask yourself the question; "Does being dazed, confused, sniffling, retreating broken shell of a human huddled in a corner, appeal to me?" If the answer to that question is NO, then zero children is your number. I was either not warned or I was not listening because we had three! With each child the occurrences of the dazed state increases, a lot! You know zero is a nice round number, it's a good number. The following rule is an absolute to be strictly adhered to. Here it is; the number of children should never be more than the number of adults in the house. If you are going to have more than two children, then an aunt, uncle, grandmother, some adult must live with you. We did not, we should have! Don't think for a moment that once they figure out that they have you out numbered that a six year old, a four year old, and a two year old can't overwhelm you and take over. You end up, well you know… that dazed state.

What does this mean to the parents? Probably they only see them at church, or the grocery store, They don't live in the house with them like you do, but everyone becomes an expert on raising YOUR kids. Maybe it was just me; maybe I had a look that said "HELP," because when I had the kids everyone wanted to give me advice. *What does this mean to the parents?* Think back on all the things you said your child would or would not do. Better yet remember those kids of other parents that you said your kid would never be like. Remember zero..good number. Get used to eating out of doggie bags. Rarely will you be able to finish a meal in a restaurant due to some unexplained screaming fit. You will notice that friends invite you over less and less. Live near relatives. The more children, the fewer the baby sitters. Three kids, no sitters, only close relatives.

What does it mean to the parents? It means you get to look at the world from a different viewpoint. Kids will make observations that will crack you up from their view. An example; Grandpa was at war with moles at the country house. The destruction to the yard is explained. On the way home, we pass a rice field that had the levees but had not been flooded. Hannah, who was five, seriously stated; "I would hate to see the mole that did that." Just shake your head and go on. It means pictures, videos, pets, endless games of whiffle ball, kiddy pool, egg hunts, musicals, Candyland, and sleep. What it means to parents is eating the cookies and drinking the milk left for Santa. It's staying up Christmas Eve to stuff the stockings. It is the smell of baby oil and lotion.

What does it mean to the parents? The first time you hear "DaDa" even twenty years later when you hear "Dad" is one of the greatest privileges in the world. It means holding out your arms coaxing them to take those first steps. It means hiding in the back rooms, jumping out, to have them let out a squeal and take off running to Mom then to do it again and again. It means camp outs in the living room under a tent made from a sheet and telling scary stories. It means all five of us in one bed for the next week due to the scary stories. It means getting to experience the trust that they believe I can do anything, especially take care of them. It means having someone love you unconditionally. It means tucking them into bed and saying night-night prayers. Talking about a window into some one's heart. It's setting around the table for hours after the meal sharing memories that they have about growing up. It's about walking into a crowded gym and having your kids spot you at the door and coming down to hug you regardless who is watching. It's about the joy of baptizing them into Christ. It's about the daily phone calls to Mom to check in. It's about our twenty year-old flopping down on the waterbed between us. It's about getting back in the waterbed. It's about having too many memories that could be recalled at one time.

Remember riding a roller coaster and reaching that point when the coaster crests the hill and falls? Remember the feeling you had in your stomach? Remember the thrills that came with each turn? You have a glimpse of having kids. You know what … three is a good number.

Chapter 16
WADING STICK

"Cliff, do you think those rapids are getting louder?" I asked as he landed another rainbow. He's not paying attention; he's too busy catching fish. You see, the MORE water that runs over the rocks the louder the noise coming from the rapids, and between several unproductive casts I had noticed the river is rising, rapidly! The ankle deep shoal that we crossed no longer exists. Just let me say, fishermen on the east side of the river, our truck on the west...

It was early June, the air still too cold for a person to be wet. I would have made it back across, dry, except for, that rock, that rock that latched on to my toe and I didn't have my wading stick. Under!..Completely! fishing pole, tackle box, and even, well, what was my LUCKY fishing hat...under! If only I had not been in such a hurry and grabbed my wading stick. I would have been dry!

God is much like my wading stick, and life is much like wading a river. I can't tell you the number of times the "stick" has been what I leaned on for stability and kept me from a colossal splash into the river. Look back in your life at the times when figuratively you were falling down, arms flailing, legs going in opposite directions, your head just about to go under. What a mess! Were you leaning on God for stability? Were you trying to go it alone?

Proverbs 3:5 Trust in the Lord with all your heart and lean not on your own understanding.

The river is full of obstacles that can be seen. Those are usually easy to get around. It is the obstacles that lie beneath the surface that often cause us to fall. It's the deep hole that we step off into. With "stick" in hand I am able to use the stick to find those hidden obstacles, I am able to safely navigate around would-be disasters. God does that for us if we would only listen. He sees what we can't see, he knows what we can't know, and he says "Don't go there"… "Don't do that"…."Watch out for_____" … "That's over your head." When we keep Stick in hand and listen, we can overcome any obstacle the devil plants for us fall on. When we don't…

Psalms 32:8 I will instruct thee and teach thee in the way which thou shalt go: I will guide thee with mine eye.

Falling in the river is not only a chilling experience it produces down right panic. You see, rushing water can have enough force that getting back up is next to impossible and drowning is a real possibility. And wading in rivers is not a matter of will I fall in; but a matter of when will I fall in! So what do you do? Easy. Have "stick" in hand which makes getting up much, much easier. We are going to fall in life. Sometimes in real swift water, and at times you are going to go completely under. Chilling? No doubt…scary…absolutely… Life or death? Could be. We try as we may to get up on our own, coughing, kicking…sinking…drowning. It can't be done, WHAT DO I DO? Take hold of the Stick; grasp it firmly and lean on it to stand again! When it's over you may be dripping wet and bruised, but you can stand again!

Isaiah 42:16 I will lead the blind by ways they have not known, along unfamiliar paths I will guide them; I will turn the darkness into light before them and make the rough places smooth. These are the things I will do; I will not forsake them.

Often when we get in calm water, we think we no longer need the Stick, or we get busy with fishing, baiting the hook, new hooks, different lure, and we …well we…we turn loose of the Stick, and the next step we take…not good! Or maybe we get too busy at the truck when we are getting ready…we're getting the important stuff, pliers, rag- don't want to get hands dirty,- net, you know, the important stuff, and we leave the Stick at the truck all together. In our haste we don't bother to bring Him along. When we feel the cold water of reality splashing in our faces then, yes, then we realize the important stuff.

The great thing about my "stick" is that it is now tied to my waders. I go fishing, I have the Stick. And if for some reason, I let go of the Stick, it's tied to me... it's not far, all I do is reach out and take it into my hand. In life we get busy, we forget, and sometimes we fall …flat.under… God is not far away. Reach out and take him into your hand, lean on him, and stand again!

Proverbs 3:21-26- [21] My son, let not them depart from thine eyes: keep sound wisdom and discretion: [22] So shall they be life unto thy soul, and grace to thy neck. [23] Then shalt thou walk in thy way safely, and thy foot shall not stumble. [24] When thou liest down, thou shalt not be afraid: yea, thou shalt lie down, and thy sleep shall be sweet. [25] Be not afraid of sudden fear, neither of the desolation of the wicked, when it cometh. [26] For the LORD shall be thy confidence, and shall keep thy foot from being taken.

The water was indeed rising. After I surfaced I went to the correct bank, the one the truck was on. Cliff???? I'll make it simple: Truck (and Stan) on the west side of river…Cliff on the east side...Bridge two mile hike in waders.

Chapter 17
POPPY AND GRANDMA

The kids, who knew so much more than they, talked them into doing it. Deep down they didn't want to. He, having been born in the 1800's, and she, having been born in the early 1900's, had spent all of their childhood and most of their adult life in homes that electricity was not available. So when Poppy and Grandma agreed to move to town it was a big deal. The first morning they lived in town Grandma got up early and cooked breakfast. She got Poppy up and as he was eating he complained that he felt really sleepy and asked what time it was. It was because Grandma woke up during the night and saw the street light and thought it was the sun. Actually it was 2 a.m. Grandma and Poppy you know I was twenty years old when someone mentioned Wolford Henson and I didn't know who they were talking about. That was when I found out they had real names.

This is about the same time I saw Grandma with her hair down. She always kept it in a bun, her hair reached her waist. She didn't have her teeth in either, scared me. One thing I did learn at an early age and anyone who visited them with me found out the same fact; and that was I am the only grandson they had, fourteen granddaughters and one grandson. Every time Kenna would visit them she was told by Poppy, "Take good care of him he's my only grandson." The move to town would save him the near two mile daily walk to town. He would walk to town to get groceries? No. To get supplies? No. He went to town to join his buddies at the square to chew and whittle and discuss. Two things I remember vividly; first, was how sharp those gentlemen kept their knives, periodically one of them would show how his knife was sharp enough to shave your arm, (fortunately that lesson was learned from observation not person experience). Poppy's knife was a Barlow which came with the Tuff-Nutt overalls that he wore daily The second lesson (learned from experience) was the length of time a seven year old remains sick after a chew of Bull O The Woods twist. Its hours. There were many other lessons I learned from them babysitting me; leave the rooster alone, leave the hens alone because of the rooster, don't throw corn cobs down the well, tomcats will kill baby kittens, butter milk does not taste like sweet milk (that courtesy of my aunt Lyndall), water captured in a rain barrel tastes better than well water, stay out of the apple tree until the apples get ripe, the trip to the moon was make believe, and wrestling was real. Walking was a way of life for Poppy. As a young adult when he had to travel from one town to the next, He did not follow the roads; he went as the crow flies. Another habit that was termed as strange was that he never had a wood pile; he got up every morning a cut the wood for the day. I think I inherited a large dose of his procrastination.

He was a physical specimen; I'm not sure how good an athlete he was, but his prowess at throwing a baseball has been confirmed by several sources. On a bet (which he won) he threw a baseball through the buckboard of a wagon, breaking the board completely in two. A scout from the Dodgers came to the Ozarks to scout the talent in the area. One of the drills was to measure how far they could throw a baseball. Poppy chose to go last, when it came his turn he got on his knees and threw the ball beyond anyone that day. He was signed to a contract to play baseball. On the day he was to leave, his parents reasoned with him that he could not make any money playing professional baseball. In today's ridiculous contracts it's hard to imagine that they were right, but they were. He stayed home to farm and later joined the army and fought in the Austria Alps during WWI. Weary from marching in the mountains, he and a fellow soldier crawled under the roof of a barn that had been blown off the structure. It provided shelter from the elements. They fell asleep and missed the fact that his company had moved out. The company was engaged in battle that was rather intense. That evening they set up camp at a new location. When they took a head count Poppy and the other soldier were assumed to be killed in action. Word was sent home by letter to the fact.

It took a couple days for them to reunite with their company and word was never sent home that he had survived. As time passed, his tour was over and he went home. He arrived home to find all the neighbors gather at his parent's home mourning his death. Due to some glitch, the letter had arrived only the day before he arrived home…alive. The history of his family is even stranger. At a time when the Native American Indians were being forced to reservations there was a local Indian Chief who had two little girls who he felt would not survive the trip. He had befriended a white family. The Chief left the two girls with the white family with the understanding that he would come back to get them when it would be possible. A couple years passed and the Chief sent someone to get his two daughters. An argument ensued that ended with the white man killing the Indian Chief's representative. The white family raised the two girls as their own. The younger of the two girls was Poppy's mother, my great grandmother.

He was very much a prankster. They lived along the Norfork River in the Arkansas Ozarks. All the farming was done along the river. Poppy would take advantage of his strong throwing arm. He would find one of his fellow farmers plowing. He would gather walnuts, get over a hill where he could not be seen and begin hurling the walnuts at his friends until the farmer would have to vacate the field. This was not malicious, just good friends aggravating each other.

Living along the Norfork river word came that the Corps of Engineers was going to build a dam, resulting in a lake. He related the worst day of his life was when the surveyors came through and put red flags where the lake's water level would be. When they looked UP to the flags in the woods they realized their home would soon be flooded. Poppy worked a couple years helping clear the land which is now Norfork Lake. They then moved to Arbyrd, Missouri.

Years later I moved to Mountain Home as a teacher but during the summers I worked as a park ranger on Norfork Lake. I had the pleasure as I toured around to meet some of Poppy's contemporaries who confirmed the stories that I had suspicion had in the past been embellished but were confirmed by these other individuals.

Chapter 18
SHAKE RATTLE AND ROLL!

Step by painfully slow step, we inched closer. Darkness and trees provided cover as we stealthily moved in. Although, when you are six feet four inches tall and weigh 260 pounds, there aren't a lot of trees to hide behind. Oh, I could hide behind them but I had to face the fact that something was going to be showing out from behind most trees, so I relied heavily on darkness. The person I was with was much smaller and experienced at this kind of situation. Oh no! Headlights…got to find a bigger tree! About ten feet away is a nice Red Oak. Having made the tree, my chances of being detected are reduced although not eliminated. The tree does not shield me completely. "Cooper; stop laughing." The Cooper is Gary Cooper, my co-worker for eight years. Gary is a legend in the Ozarks around Salem, Viola, and Highland. You will hear him referred to as "Sarge" due to his flattop that he wore, or "the old coach". Gary was a math teacher and ex-coach. He was one of the first summer rangers that the Corps of Engineers at Mt. Home hired and worked for them for over thirty summers. People who camped at Lake Norfork always wanted to know if "Coop" was working. They, probably being the victim of one of his jokes, stories, or card tricks. If you were lucky enough for Gary to call you by your real name it was always your last name: Johnson, Estes, Oliver, or Fancher for example. He had nicknames for the people who were closest to him. For three years I went thinking his wife's name was Sally until someone told me her real name, Wilma. Gary was also known for his sayings. "Skipping through the dew" meant someone was driving too fast. "We are going to get some of his popcorn money" meant we were going to write that person a ticket. Gary was forever telling us "young bucks" that we did not know what we were doing; it did not matter what the situation was. One night it happened…we "young bucks" have never laughed as hard as the night Gary was showing us "young bucks" how to properly put an injured possum out of its pain. When the contents of the possum's colon spewed out onto his shirt we "young bucks" have yet to contain our laughter to this day some twelve years later.

Now we are in search of the source of some very loud music. In the campgrounds, quiet hours begin at 10 p.m., this music was "knocking the acorns off the trees." (Another saying of Gary's) and it was midnight. This was the tent section, wooded, and somewhat secluded. Step by, um, stealthy step (another fact…260 pound people can't walk quietly through the woods) we get within ten feet of the source and they do not know that we are even anywhere around. All they would have had to do was look up and they would have seen one of us only partially hidden. Astounding best describes what we observed. First was the loud music playing "Shake Rattle and Roll" then there are two spot lights shining on this campsite that would rival the illumination of the sun. Three girls about thirty, two of them are preparing the tents; the third facing the road rolling a small pile of marijuana cigarettes. Yes you read that correctly, marijuana cigarettes. What else could they have done to draw attention to themselves, flashing lights? They thought they were hidden and all was good. Imagine their surprise when we stepped out from behind the trees. They stood there guilty, caught red handed, trying to explain the bag and pile away.

It seems that many people live their lives this way. We get so busy with the stuff of living and we don't bother to look up and acknowledge that God is there. No not there, he is here close to us. We may commit sins that we think are hidden and we are lulled into believing that all is good. In fact, to God we have the loud music going and the spot lights shining on us completely illuminating all that we do. Guilty, red handed, no doubts. People are exposed everyday that we believed to be righteous only to find out that they were not serving God. Did they not bother to look up and see God here, seeing?

"Pass the biscuits" meant something out of the ordinary, or overwhelming, or astounding, or exasperating just happened.

Gary repeating the story laughingly would say: "You should have seen Johnson trying to hide behind a little old oak tree… pass the biscuits."

If boys are going to make it in this world they need quality men in their lives. The guidance they need does not go away when they get past the teen years. If young men are going to make it in this world, they too, need quality men in their lives. This "young buck" considers it a blessing to have spent eight summers with Gary Cooper learning many of life's lessons by the way he lives his life.

Chapter 19
WHAT A TALENT!

I think it is on the twelfth chromosome (about a third of the way down) the correct combination of proteins produce this talent. I had a way, a knack for it. It was foolproof, and it never failed. My friends did not possess the talent level that I had. This was evident by the fact that they continued to practice after my lot was cast. What I had a talent for was that every time (and I mean every time) I did something stupid I got caught. My friends did not have this talent; they, in fact, had the opposite gene, the one that allows you to get away with everything. The discovery of this gene was made long before DNA testing so my conclusions are based on observations that some of them continually did things without getting caught, and me…always caught. Some of the stupid things I did were spur of the moment, not well thought out actions. Many seemed like good ideas at the time. Some of them were pondered for a considerable amount of time, but I would still not classify them as well thought out. It seemed at the time that the only beneficiaries of these talents were my parents, teachers, and other adults who were responsible for my well being.

There had to be an indicator of some kind that allowed my parents to know immediately when I walked in the house that I was guilty. It was as if I had a neon flashing sign visible only to adults that said GUILTY. Take for example the *We're Just Looking at the Moon Incident*. I'm 16 and it is Saturday night and I get permission to go cruise town with the warning: "Do not go out of the city limits." The town was Marmaduke, three streets running north and south and every bit of …ooh…4 blocks long. It was 1977, and you can just imagine how much excitement there was in this metropolis of a thousand people. *Do not leave the city limits;* why there was barely enough room to turn my red, four-door, 1967 Ford LTD, around inside the city limits. Today, my 1967, red, four-door, Ford LTD would really be cool to drive through town in, maybe even in a few parades, but at age 16 a red, four door, 1967 Ford LTD is not cool. Did I mention that because of another stupid stunt of mine, I drove my car two years without reverse? At town I would get with the Beggs brothers, their sister and her boyfriend. We get in Richey's two door, Ford Maverick with dual exhaust, wide tires and jacked up rear end…cool car. We cruise the streets of Marmaduke until dark, even went to the A&G for a burger, then we would head for Starnes gravel pit. Need I say this was outside the city limits? Starnes gravel pit is not a place that you just happen upon, it is out of the way and today I would have a hard time remembering how to get there. So if you are at Starnes gravel pit, you have a purpose to be there. We would pull along side our friends who were already parked there, get out and discover it is not our friends but of all people it is my Aunt Lyndall and Uncle Ad. *"We just came out to look at the moon."* they said when asked what they were doing. They are in their late fifties, no kids at home, good grief is the moon not shining at their house? There it is that gene working; of all the places to go out of the city limits, and of all the places for a couple to go look at the moon they had to be one in the same. My only hope is that they will not mention this to my parents Sunday morning. At home I walk in. Dad is sitting in his recliner reading. He looks over his glasses and says; "Where did you go tonight?" A thousand questions he could have asked, how do they do that, he must know. This was pre-cell phones; it's that wonderful talent I have. I confessed.

Let me say that I could fill up a book of examples of this talent working but I will share only one more. I will call this the *May Queen Incident.* My high school, Crowley's Ridge Academy, had a May Day festival every spring. There were two May poles to which streamers were attached and the maids would wind the streamers around the pole. A queen would be chosen then she and the other seven maids would preside over the rest of the festivities sitting in rot iron white decorative lawn furniture. Cold sweat breaks out...not then... right now, recounting this deed. Reason? The lady in charge of the festivities had to be perfect and was not one to make unhappy. Wiping sweat away! Eight boys were chosen to carry the eight chairs out to the May pole with the instructions on how to arrange them. This was Friday afternoon and the festivities would be Saturday morning. When I sat mine down, from carrying it over my head, the back leg hit the ground at just the right angle that it snapped the leg off the chair; not cracked, off. I am standing there holding a wounded chair with its leg lying dead in the grass. I'm dead… lady in charge…panic...look around…no one saw. It was one of those spur of the moment decisions. Seemed like a good idea at the time. Monday morning at 8:06 I was summoned to the superintendent's office, school started at 8:05. Mr. Austin said nothing except, "Why did you do it?" Now how could he know, there were eight of us. It's that talent I have, busted, I confessed. I was not there but rumor was that the propped up leg did not hold when the queen sat down. Remember it was a back leg, get the picture.

Now that I'm older and have children of my own, I have come to realize that there was a tendency for bad luck when I was doing something I should not be doing. Mostly though it was parents, aunts, uncles, teachers, administrators, church members who cared enough about me to ask the right questions. "Where did you go?" "Why did you do it?" I think back and neither one of them knew that I had done wrong. They knew I was capable and were asking the right questions. In the case of the queen, it was obvious that one of eight boys had messed up.

I have to wonder why he started with me. Children and teens need adults in their lives who are willing and caring enough to ask the right questions.

You read in the Bible as Jesus went about his ministry when he wanted to get his point across, when he really wanted to drive it home, he often did so by asking a question or questions. He avoided the traps of the Pharisees by asking them questions. The adulterous woman, the Samaritan woman at the well, Peter, the woman who touched his garment, example after example where Jesus gave the people what they needed…a question. One of the last questions recorded was Jesus sharing a meal by the sea with a few of his apostles. He asks Peter three different ways "Do you love me?" A question that you and I answer each day.

No reverse, you had to be careful where you parked. What amazes me that at my adult age I can still do some really stupid things. Am I alone?

Chapter 20
YOU NEVER KNOW
WHERE IT WILL GO!

Your influence you never know where it will go. A cure for cancer…maybe, a new source of energy…could be, increased productivity…without a doubt. Who knows what could be discovered, invented, or improvement would occur if we all would practice this one thing. Not to mention that the world would be just a better place to live. Influence, we touch the lives of hundreds of people every day. With some people we have a large influence spending a large amount of time with them; with others the interaction may be only a fraction of a second. Either way, every contact you have with another person you leave a little piece of yourself with that person that remains and affects him forever. Hundreds a day; the lady at the drive through, the man across from you at the four-way stop, a family member, a co-worker, the possibilities out number the stars. Let that sink in, every interaction a piece of you is left behind to influence forever, may be large…may be small, but it's there…forever. When we get to the end it's all going to be about influence. What would happen to the world if each of us made a conscience effort to leave every person that we interact with a better person than they were before they interacted with us? That would be every person you met however brief would leave your presence a better person from the piece of you that you have left with them…forever.

Listen carefully, read each description carefully. Finish the story, go back and read it again, it is too important to miss. It can be brief or extended. It can be subtle as a wisp of a breeze, or it can be of the magnitude of smashing your finger with a hammer. It can be unpredictable, never knowing the path it will take, or how far it will go. Good and bad. It may seem insignificant to you but you do not know how large an impact it will have. It has a tendency to multiply. You can not get around being a part of it. You often do it and don't even know it. You are a result of it yourself. The influence you have on others becomes a part of their influence thereby multiplying. The one thing that little attention is given is the fact that once out there it is eternal it does not go away. It is everlasting with results beyond your scope.

It was one of those meetings that told us more is going to be expected from us and the sanctions are going to be greater. I enter the restaurant, practically empty, good, so I go to the far wall where there are only two tables, and that wall was away from everyone. My intentions were to ponder what next, just want to eat and be left alone. Because the restaurant is practically empty, anyone who comes in can sit where they won't be in that imaginary circle that surrounds us we call our personal space. They come in the door look around, two elderly women. They are dressed like this was a special occasion for them to be out eating. Their attire; my guess was their Sunday-go-to-church best from the late 70's. The older lady was aided by a walker, with the other graciously helping her. What is this! They are coming to sit at the table directly behind me. Good grief, "um my personal space thing here" "look around seats everywhere" I'm thinking… as they move closer. There was not enough room for her to sit right behind me which meant that I was going to have to move to the other side of the table. I would also be facing their table and would no longer be wrapped alone in my world. They were not malicious on their choice of tables, I just happened to be next to their table, the one that they always sit at. They were not bothered by me sitting near their table. Both tables are brought the hushpuppies and I watch and listen to these two ladies. They were so glad to be in one another's company. They were so glad to be out eating. They basically were soaking in life. Watching and listening there were times that I had to fight laughing out loud. At one point the eldest of the two leans over to her companion shoulders raised, huge smile, eyes squinting, giggling, whispering as if she were telling the companion that she had a crush on the new orderly at the nursing home, or something similar, she patted the hushpuppy on her plate and said as if it was top secret; "I'm saving that one to eat with my fish." No worries, just full of joy. They are making my day and they don't even know it. I enjoyed my meal and had a different attitude the rest of the day. I left the presence of those two ladies that I had never seen before or since, a better person. Who knows what effect I had on someone else the rest of the day with my renewed spirit. Increased accountability… so what, more sanctions…who cares!

You never know where it's going to go.

Jesus spent his life doing this very thing. Person by person was made better by having an encounter with Jesus. Some of the more obvious was the widow's son, Lazarus, Jarius daughter, all raised from the dead. Obviously they were made better. What about the woman at the well? What about the two men he walked with along the road? What about the young boy whose lunch fed the thousands? What about us, today? We need to encounter Jesus on a daily basis so that we may become better people. We need to learn more about him so that he can have a greater influence on our lives. By our actions, however great or small, we need to determine to make each person we contact better once they leave our company. You never know where it's going to go.

Chapter 21
LEAVING YOUR MARK

Five hundred years from now archeologist are going to be digging outside of Marmaduke and find round discs that look something like pies, but they will have been made out of dirt. By that time making mud pies will be unknown to the children of that era. In times past, hours of play were spent making mud pies. Kenna in a repentant attitude tells the story of she and her friend making mud pies and getting(making) her little sister to eat them. Summertime not only meant that school was out, that the jeans become cut offs, (this was not a waste, the knees were gone and by summer they were two inches short anyway). The Chuck Taylor's I wore to school became swimming shoes for Slavens Creek, and it also meant that cousins would be coming to visit. Dad was one of ten living children so there was no shortage of company during the summers. When the usual summer activites of baseball, horseback riding, plunking tin can with our bb guns, and skinny dipping got boring we would start using our imaginations. You can guess where that led; often to the woodshed for a lesson from one of our parents and even a few visits to the emergency room. Being younger than most of my cousins, and less traveled than all of them, I was a tad gullible. You know, I wonder if Manuel and Archie have repentant attitudes when they tell their stories of mud pies? Nonetheless, I have forgiven them. We would from time to time create a club, complete with officers, clubhouse, criteria for entry into the club, and a stamp with our symbol. The symbol was usually a letter because they are easy to carve out of a potato. So five hundred years from now when archeologist finds our mud pies they will have an imprint from the potato stamp. Things have progressed a little; at work I have my signature on a self inking permanent stamp. My signature does two things: one, it states that what I have stamped is correct and secondly, it gives them someone to blame if something goes wrong.

My grandfather was born in eighteen ninety-three and he could neither read nor write. When he had to sign something he made a mark that was unique to him. To someone in New York that mark would mean nothing, but to the people, banks, and merchants around Marmaduke that mark meant Wolford Henson. His mark was legal and binding and is probably could be found today in vaults of banks or shelves of some old store.

Physically, personality traits, discoveries, beliefs, spirituality, and education are a few of the areas or ways that we try to leave our mark or put our stamp on something. It is a big thing to be able to put your stamp on something. Stradivarius stamped his way into violin making, Rembrandt left his mark in the art world, Beethoven in music, Newton in science (maybe snacks). All these are significant, and changed the way of thinking in each discipline, changed the way things are done forever, and as long as there are schools, children will be learning about these individuals. None of these are as significant, as eternal, as far-reaching, as great an honor as leaving your mark, leaving your stamp by being a father. Not the fact that another human being's DNA is one half yours. I'm not talking about leaving your stamp on the world by simply being able to father offspring. The significant, eternal, far-reaching, honorable thing I'm talking about is being a Dad. I can't think of a greater honor bestowed on a man that to hear the words "Daddy" coming from a child when they are two year old, a teenager, a bride being given away, need advice, need money, just need to talk, and especially when they say, "Daddy, I love you." The Stradivariuses, Rembrandts, Beethoven's, and Newton's of fatherhood are rare. On February 27, 1961 I was blessed to be born to a father who has devoted his life leaving his mark in many ways which will have eternal rewards, but as many of you can say about your father, I consider mine among the best of fathers...yes and more important a Rembrandt of a Dad. I have the honor of having three children that call me... for advice, often for money, best of all they call me Dad and it is my prayer that I will be their Beethoven.

Since Archie and Manuel were the oldest they got to be president of the club, therefore all the mud pies had an A or an M. Come to think of it archeologist aren't going to find our mud pies, after they baked in the sun they made great ammo for the dirt clod fights.

Chapter 22
GIVE ME GRAVEL

Get in your car, turn on the radio to a country station and in less than three minutes you will hear a song about them or at the least a reference to them in a song. They are disappearing daily. Once they are gone it is very doubtful that they will be back. I imagine there are people in big cities that have never seen one in real life. What a shame! The crazy thing about this is that many people in different counties have raised taxes on themselves to help exterminate them. Some people despise them, but I, for one, think they were a blessing. Gravel roads, regrettably, are disappearing at an alarming rate. In the name of progress they are being buried under a thick layer of some petroleum derived product. This is being done at an enormous cost financially and to the health of our society. Few things can be directly linked to the decline of our nation like the paving of country roads.

What was supposed to better our lives by making it cleaner and efficient has failed miserably. Can you see the roads I am talking about? The ones that look like an ever narrowing tunnel as you look down the length of the road. They looked like a tunnel from the Catalpa and Persimmon trees that lined the sides of the roads, growing to meet at the top forming a canopy with their broad green leaves and long seed pods. You might see someone collecting the best catfish bait known to the southern angler; catalpa worms. They are caterpillars that infest the trees at certain time of the year. They must be to catfish what chocolate is to people, catfish gobble them up. Collection equipment was a long pole to knock them out of the trees and a container to put them in. Sure enough there is Mr. Hill gathering his bait. Passing by on a gravel road, you are likely to stop and talk with him probably for an extended time building a bond, and you might get a catfish supper out of the conversation. Today you're going so fast that IF someone were brave enough to do this collecting on a paved road you would probably zip right on by. Gravel country roads. It was the golden era of the "two finger" wave. With hand draped over the top of the steering wheel, as a car approaches the index and middle finger are raised together to form a wave that was done to every car you met. This is a lost art causing the world to be a less friendly world all due to the paved road. Thursday after work you're going down the gravel road to your house, arm out the window, Mr. Redwine is out in his garden, you honk, and he waves you to stop by, so you pull into his driveway. An hour later many of the world's problems have been solved, the preacher has been fired and you are on your way home with a grocery bag full of produce. That doesn't happen on a paved road…too fast, honk-wave-pass…all at the same time, so problems go unsolved, more bad sermons from the preacher, and people become more isolated; paved roads… arr. If you lived at the end of the road, they served as warning signals that somebody was coming to the house to visit. Many times last minute straightening had to be done once we saw the cloud of dust traveling towards us. With paved roads you don't know they are coming until they are knocking at the door; no chance to pick up, so they see the real condition of the living room. Look at the rates on automobile insurance and you will see an increase in prices as the miles of gravel roads decreases. Today's new drivers are not as good as those that grew up during the gravel road glory days. Where else can a ten year old child sit in his parent's lap and learn to steer a vehicle, and in the years that follow learn to control the gas and brakes? I know, I know that it was illegal to allow children that young to drive on public roads but they were gravel roads. The parent child relation is not the same when learning to drive on paved roads versus the relationship while learning to drive on gravel roads. With the faster pace of paved roads the relationship is much more strained, parents are under more stress as they teach their children to drive. For many families the stress is too great so either the child or the parent decides not to partake in the bonding activity and the teen/parent gap widens. With gravel roads learning to drive was more laid back activity for teen/

parent. Another thing that children are missing out on is the chance to ride in the back of a pickup. Much too dangerous to do at the high speeds of paved roads but turn onto a gravel road, stop the truck, and jump in the back. If it happens to be one of the days that you are not learning to drive. But before you get in the back of the truck you stock up on one very important item that the gravel roads just happen to have a limitless supply of …rocks. Trees, cans, and I have to admit an occasional mail box became the target of many a young boy riding in the back of a pickup on a gravel road. Do you realize how much science there is in learning to get the right trajectory to hit a target out of the back of a moving pickup? I wonder how many scientists that work for NASA grew up on gravel roads? Talk about something special; driving slow enough that it's safe for your girl friend to sit next to you with your right arm around her and your left hand draped over the top of the steering wheel at the wrist ready to give the cool "two finger" wave to anyone you meet. It's great if you meet your best friend who is in his pick up… by himself. And we think paved roads are progress. I did not find this action to be so special when I happened behind my daughter sitting like this in her boyfriends Jeep going down the road. Listening to the older generation talk about the weather during their early years, I had always thought it snowed more back then. The difference instead is the gravel roads; the snow stayed on those roads longer than the black paved roads of today. Snow covered gravel roads meant no school for the children, for many days in a row not the one or two scattered days we miss now.

Life is too fast now, too hectic.

So get your spouse or child, drive until you find an out of the way gravel road, sit close to each other…then roll down the window and ease slowly along. Enjoy the flowers that we zip past on paved roads, enjoy the squirrels and other wild life you may see. Enjoy the pace, the time, the memories, and the company. Just don't be throwing rocks; I understand they really frown on that. So there was a little dirt that collected in the car and house from the gravel roads. So it took you longer to go to the grocery store. I place the de-graveling of our roads right up there with the de-forestation of the rain forest. Who needs pavement…give me gravel.

Chapter 23
Dinosaurs

Some people want to go to the movies to be scared out of their wits…not me. Others go to cry, walk out with tears streaming down both cheeks and say, "wasn't that a great movie"…not me. Still others like the challenge of a mystery with twists and turns that causes the viewer to engage in analytical thinking during the movie, and often times know less at the end than in the beginning… not me. On the rare occasion that I go to the movie I just want to sit there be entertained and laugh a little or better yet a lot. One of my favorite movies is *Men in Black*. Every time I watch it I see something new that I missed in the previous times I have watched it. I am amazed at the creativity of the individuals who created this movie. I don't know their names but can see a frustrated mother of those boys. I bet she has a permanent twitch in her right eye. Another movie idea that I liked was *Jurassic Park.* Notice I said I like the idea of the movie, the movie itself was much too stressful, but I like the science behind the movie and I like dinosaurs, all those creatures with long funny sounding names. Dinosaurs living among us today raise some intriguing questions; what would church pot lucks be like, T.Rex. Stew anyone? Would it be the St. Louis Pterodactyls? Would the Chicago Trilobites have won a world series by now, or most importantly which ones taste like chicken? One thing that I took from the movie was that dinosaurs would wreak havoc on the world that we are accustomed to today. Can you imagine the traffic jam should a *Brachiosaurs* decide to browse the vegetation along side a major interstate with it's enormous tail blocking all lanes of traffic? Although the idea of dinosaurs living today is intriguing, they would be too much trouble. The dinosaurs that people like are the ones that are extinct and cause us no trouble.

There seems to be among any group; church, school, work, you name the group and you will find a dinosaur in the group. Just like the real dinosaurs would wreak havoc in today's world these living dinosaurs cause enormous harm to individuals and whatever group or organization they are around. They have been studied and determined to have characteristics that are too detrimental to be allowed to exist. These dinosaurs need to be buried in an undisclosed location so that they would never be found again. That is the characteristics not the person themselves. So if you see a person with a shovel trying to dig to find the location of one of these dinosaurs; encourage them to put the shovel down, lovingly take it away from them, and if they persist and persist, well I guess you have to hit them with their own shovel. Have you seen any of these dinosaurs hanging around? *Unhappiness negativitus, Itsgottobe mywayus, Thatwillus neverworkitis?* Or maybe this pair of closely related species; *Harmfullus backbitis and Harmfullus gossippitis.* Get the idea…that is, if you understand homemade Latin? You could probably come up with some of your own. Don't use spell check; mine shorted out trying to figure out those names. These dinosaurs may be solitary animals or they may travel in groups. Just like real dinosaurs they can be big and cumbersome, a load to drag alone, they weigh you down. Others are hidden, great at camouflage, fast as lighting. They come in, do their damage and are gone before you know what happened. Have you seen these?

The good news is that there are some newly discovered species. They are refreshing, beneficial to all they come in contact with. They are some of the most beautiful creatures that have ever been created. Some of them are: *Teamworkus supportallofus, Benificialus joyitis, Complainitis nonexisticus, Arguetis gonus.* These species although rare do exist as well as do others that are good. They are fragile and need to be handled with care. These species are slow growing they emerge over a long time. These species need to be cultivated and encouraged to be passed on to other people, lest they become extinct. Have you seen these species around?

Searching for these characteristics, one should not go far to examine the existence of one of the dinosaur or one of the new species, may just take a look in the mirror. So if you find yourself holding a shovel with the urge to dig up dinosaurs, lay it down, slowly back away, and go see a comedy.

Chapter 24
DEPENDENCE
ON
?

It starts to show at an early age, about when a baby begins to walk and talk, that's when it really becomes apparent, thus the "terrible two". A little girl I know well (she is my wife's third child) had her Sunday church clothes laid out for her by her mother to wear that morning to church.

There are events that happen in your life that remain as clear years later as if they happened today. This is one of those events. Hannah came walking through the kitchen with a pair of slime green biker shorts, with a tee shirt that was purple to match. Kenna cooking breakfast looked at her and told her that she couldn't wear that to church. As I think about what happened next I am finding it amusing, but it was not at that time. She put her little hand on her hip and said, "it's my body and I'll wear what I want to wear". She was two and a half years old. Rarely did it happen, but Kenna snapped and the conversation went something like this, with spatula waving for emphasis, "That body came from this body and this body is still in charge of that little body." Daddy's little girl sure looked pretty that morning in that pink ruffle dress and bow in her hair. Multiply that incident times three children and this would not be the last encounter over the next 16 years. It also would not be the last snap by these three children's parents.

A lot of us have it built into our personalities. Males get a double dose. And to be frank, Americans, for the most part, really possess these characteristics. We want to do what we want to do, when we want to, where we want to, and without the help or guidance from anyone. So in short, what I'm saying is that we are independent, self sufficient, self reliant, be in charge types. How ridiculous not to listen to those who can help us, those who know. When our babies were born I knew how to raise children, I had read the books, observed others raising their children and declared to the world what our children would not do. I continue to be amused by those statements. Why don't we depend on the experienced, the capable, the willing?

Have you ever been in a situation where you were totally reliant on another person? A situation where there would be a major impact on your wellbeing and the outcome is not in your hands. Four years ago Kenna and I decided to take a vacation to a resort town in Mexico. Now this was big for us because of our limited travel experiences. Any travel we had done had been with a group. This would be our first time out of the United States together, and it would be our first time to navigate an airport by ourselves. This was big for two people who rarely had been out of Arkansas. We were green; we were so green that if you planted us we would have grown. After a couple of days we had ventured away from the motel enough to feel comfortable with the bus system. So we decided to ride the bus for its entire loop that the map showed it took. We boarded the bus at the stop in front of the motel. Our choice of times illuminated our ignorance; it was five p.m. I don't know what percent of the native workforce uses the bus system but for the exception of about nine other tourists that entire percentage was on that bus. Rush hour. We were enjoying seeing the new landscapes you couldn't see from our motel room. The Bus stops at the market; several exit, one or two more stops and several more exit, a stop at the eating establishments more exit. The door closes and the bus goes in motion and I realize two things. We are now the only tourists left on the bus, and the bus at five p.m. takes a different route than the one posted. We have turned to the residential area. And not a very good part of the residential area to say the least. I could tell we were not in Arkansas any longer. This was confirmed by a young lady who had been sleeping in the seat across from us. She awoke, looked around and asked in a tone of amazement, "Where are you trying to go?" We smiled a perky little smile and said in a happy, we don't know what we are doing tone of voice, "We are going to ride the bus the entire loop back to the motel." "NO!" was her immediate rather forceful reply. "You should not be here," she continued. She wore a maid's uniform which indicated she supposedly was employed by one of the many resorts. She stood up as the bus came to a stop and said, "Come with me I will get you on the next bus back to the motel." The area she asked us to get off the bus was one of broken glass lying every where, bars on every window, and graffiti on all the buildings. She seemed sincere but who knows what she could be setting us up for. Who knows what danger lies ahead should we stay on the bus. She looked at us and said, "I will not leave you". At that moment we placed our well being into that young girl's hands. We were lost, in a foreign country, and totally dependant on her. She took us across the road and we waited on a returning bus. Several passed that we would have boarded but she waited for the one that went back to our motel. When the bus stopped, she stepped up to the driver and I wish I knew what she told the driver in Spanish but when she finished the driver waved us unto the bus, and get this, would not take our fare. The young girl said, "You be okay now" smiled, waved bye, and got off the bus. The driver had us sit in the front and narrated how many more stops to our motel. I am convinced I have met one of my guardian angels. She was living in Cancun, and working at a resort. Her name is Maria, and I sincerely thank God she rides the five p.m. bus home. We were in a totally dependant situation.

Do we not find ourselves in the same situation? By the very fact that life here on earth is temporary and our home is being prepared in heaven, we are therefore in a foreign land, left alone to our own abilities we find ourselves lost, without hope. Jesus came wearing the uniform of a servant. He has asked each one of us to follow him and he has promised "I will not leave you." To commit to follow him means total dependence on him.

When I got back to the motel I looked in a Spanish/English dictionary to see if I could find any of the conversation that Maria had with the bus driver. I recognized the word "tourist" which was okay, but "helpless dummies"?

Chapter 25
BEAU

When Jesus chose his apostles at least four of them were fishermen. Jesus, it seems, spent a lot of time around the water, sometimes in a boat, but at least once, he even took a stroll on the water. That's at least one thing Jesus and I have in common. Oh, not the walking on water but liking to be around water.

As a kid did you ever wish you could do supernatural things like being able to fly, or have super strength? I think walking on water would have been a great one. Even as an adult? Think about it. You pull down to the river, grab your gear, and take off to your favorite spot. No cumbersome waders, and those rocks that have been under running water can be very, very slippery…not to worry. This would give you the advantage over that annoying fisherman who watches you catch a couple fish then moves right to the spot you were fishing. This would allow you to get close enough to…to kick water on him and run. (I think you could get forgiveness for that). Or you happen to hook a ten pound trout (they say those exist although I would have to personally say they do not) on line designed to catch much smaller trout. The catch of your life swims too fast up stream and breaks your line. Your only possible consolation is that someone was fishing with you and can confirm the near record catch or else you dare not tell anyone and perpetuate the gross misconception that all fishermen are stretchers of the truth. If you walk on water, it becomes a chase increasing the odds that you will be able to net the fish, estimate the weight and turn it loose. Later you are recounting the story to less fortunate fishermen on how you walked on water, recounting every turn up stream then down. You tell how you just happened to have your scales that day and it was ten pounds three ounces. Through all the time you know what they will be interested in…"Where did you catch it?"

If you take someone fishing with you for the purpose of validating your stories, take a kid. However big you want the catch to be that's what you tell the kid and they will eagerly relay it to everyone. Nothing like starting them off early learning to tell… well …fish tales. One of my favorite fishing partners is Beau Horn. Beau was five when I started fishing with him, along with his Dad and his brothers. So Beau is in pre-school teaching me a few things about fishing and life's circumstances. Beau is passionate about fishing. He can sit still for hours and talk about fishing. He knows a lot about fishing, power bait, rooster tails, and brands of waders and where to fish. Other kids bring their coloring books to church Beau brings his Cabela's catalogue. Oh, if only we adults had something that meant that much to us. Things that should bubble that kind of passion to the surface, church, family, heaven. Beau would stand beside me holding the bait patiently waiting. A fish would steal our bait (must be a ten pounder messing with my heart) and he would have the next bait ready to put on the hook. For him that was fishing, and the excitement when I would hook one. He would be equally excited when one of his brothers would catch one. I guess he would be should his Dad catch one. Wow! How many of us are willing to be in the background doing what needs to be done for good to succeed. Don't most of us want to be the one that is reeling in the fish? It's the rare person that gets down right giddy when someone else succeeds. One day Beau and I had fished for 11/2 hours and not gotten a single bite. We had used all our bait, tried every lure we had. A year later writing this I am laughing at what he asked me. He said, "Mr. Stan, how many is it we can keep before we have to start throwing them back?" Did you catch what I said? Over an hour…no bites on all the bait we had used, and Beau is convinced that we are going to have to throw some back. Give me a big gulp of that optimism. When all is stacked against you, having used all your resources, and still being convinced that everything will be good, and you may have to throw some back.

Some of the "other" things I learned: You don't have to be still and quiet to catch fish. You don't stop at Sonic and give kids a Route 44 drink when they will be putting on waders. Kids do not run out of questions. They don't understand water depth and top of their waders (which when the cold water goes below the waistline that complicates the rt. 44 thing) Finally, uncontrolled shivering and blue lip does not mean you are cold!

We managed to catch some trout. How many Beau? Right…35. And how big was the smallest one? Correct again, 3 pounds. Now they're going to ask you where you caught them and what do you say? ……That's right we caught them in the lips.

Chapter 26
WET MATCHES!

They make it look so easy on television. They make you think any one can do it. I guess these companies pay advertising agencies big bucks to make it look that way. And another thing that really gets me is the way they appeal to the male ego. No, I mean that one really does get me every time. I fall for it and it is sooo annoying. I bet there are many of you men have been hooked also. Some time around your birthday or father's day, or even Christmas you volunteer to go with your wife to get milk and you subtly lead them right by the newest "must have" boost my ego gadget. Never mind this gadget being on the opposite end of the mega store. This is a calculated risk taken by the man, though, because between your new gadget and the milk is a whole vast number of items that you are now going to be exposed to that appeal to her. I'm being careful here…we men possibly would view them as vain, but, men you should never, ever make fun of or criticize the amount of "necessary" things she has. Chances are you will do something to destroy one of those things and be accused of forever after of doing it on purpose…something like the number of pairs of shoes she may possess.

Spring cleaning was performed over spring break one year. The entire throw away stuff was bagged up and boxed up ready to be hauled off. I promise I did not know! I promise that I was totally unaware that Kenna was switching her winter shoes to another closet and that the really big , really heavy ,(hurt my back moving it), biggest box I'd ever seen, sitting by our bedroom door was supposed to go in the closet not the…You should never tease about how much. To this day she thinks I did that on purpose. The next winter, guess what store we went to every time we went to get milk? With three teenagers it sure seemed like we were always going to get milk!

I would not be surprised to find out that a number of men out there have stooped lower. Sometime around your birthday, Father's day, or Christmas you volunteered to go get milk, and under the pretense of letting your wife rest, you talk her into staying at home. You return home later with a gallon of milk and a new Brinks Charcoal Smoker Grill Combination and you very lovingly say, "See what you got me for Father's Day." Then you explain the ease with which you can produce a variety of culinary wonders because you have been watch cooking channels on satellite TV (my birthday present). They make it look so easy. It is not. My smoker was "given" to me before there were gas smokers, before the easy light charcoal. Remember, before those handy little butane lighters you had matches. The early attempts were times of burned knuckles, and singed eyebrows, that lighter fluid is funny stuff. There is a certain order of events one should follow when lighting charcoal.

I learned about matches at an early age from swimming at Slaven's creek. The connection between the two are explained in another story titled *Smoked Grapevine Burned Tongue.* Matches come in three common types. The largest of the matches is the kitchen match. These are the ones made out of wood and are extra thick and long. These are the best, rub them on any rough surface and they burst into duty. I've seen them ignited on jeans, boots, hitching post (John Wayne) and teeth (Archie and Manuel). They burn for a longer time allowing the user the greatest window to accomplish their task. Then there is the smaller version of the kitchen match. Again ready to burst into service at any time. Being shorter the burning power is not as great, although while burning they can do considerable amount of good. Then there are the paper matches, short, flimsy, come all hooked together with the other matches you have to tear it away from the other paper matches before using. These matches are more difficult to use due to the fact that they have to be ignited on just the right surface. Rub them on the correct surface and watch out here they go! They don't burn as long but still doing good while they burn. The uses for all these matches are limitless, the number of lives saved could not be counted, lives made better by matches.

It's cold, hands are shaking. He has got to get a fire going to dry his wet clothes…this could be life threatening. Lost, he needs to start a fire to signal his location. Hungry kids will eat cold soup, but it would taste better hot. Darkness remains if there is no light. You see, matches were created to be used and used rather quickly. The longer they sit around, the harder they are to ignite. You see there is something that renders the match useless and that is water. Matches can draw moisture from being unused or some event can occur that gets the match wet. (Such as a rainstorm while trying to cook burgers). All of us have had the experience of desperately needing a match only to have the head of the match fall off and smear on the striking surface. The match looks good, but it does not fulfill what it was created for. We were created for a purpose we were intended to be used. It does not matter what kind of match you are as long as you don't become a wet match.

Hey it's two weeks to my birthday! I yell down the hall "Honey when you finish what you are doing sit down and rest, I'm going to get milk"

Now wait a minute, what's this box doing by the door?

Chapter 27
The Waiting Season

Sometime shortly after Halloween it would come in the mail and its arrival would mark the beginning of the *waiting season*. It. was the Sears Christmas Catalogue, a book made just for the kids. Gone out of this catalogue were those sections that wasted good paper, the shoes, clothes, household items, and automotive section, all gone. What was left was a collection of the finest toys, gadgets, and necessities ever collected into one book. Hot Wheels complete with track and carrying case, Pogo Sticks, BB Guns, Tonka Trucks, Bikes, and so much more, all within a few color filled pages. The only flaw this catalogue had was that for some crazy reason someone decided to leave the doll section in...what a waste. This time of year it was okay to be envious of the kid who was the only child. They would not have to share the catalogue. Hours spent looking at each page, decisions, wishes, hope, anticipation; and dreams. all added together…wow that was a good time! Kids looked at those so much that they began to take ownership of the catalogue. In time it would have marks and turned down pages…all clues to the "Bearded One", and being forced to share this catalogue with others puts in jeopardy any hope of the "Bearded One" getting which toy belonged to which kid in the family. The thought would flash through my mind…my sister…the doll section…he would never do that, would he? Once one took possession of that catalogue the Christmas season officially had began, for a youngster the most exciting time of the year, the *waiting season*. It seems to me that Christmas may have lost some of its power to cause the high level of excitement that it once did. Now I admit this may be a result of me being forty-six instead of six and on the buying end instead of on the receiving end. I think it's more because the season starts in August now. The excitement, and the wait is spread out over such a long time that it is different now.

Christmas now and Christmas then is much like watching Mr. Lentz clear stumps out of a field that at one time was a forest. Two methods as I remember were used, one was soak the stump with some flammable liquid and set it on fire, the results were not spectacular, the stump would burn then smolder for days as it slowly burned away. Thus should be Christmas today, a warm glow, spread out over time before it gradually disappears. The second method of removal was dynamite; no I mean it really was dynamite!

The dynamite complete with fuse would be packed under the stump. When he would light that fuse the wait started, and the anticipation, and excitement complete with racing heart beat, sweaty palms…short lived, but there was tremendous excitement ending with chunks of stump flying through the air. The deafening sound, and the dirt cloud all added to the excitement of that stump being removed. Thus was Christmas from the past, the excitement would build as the decorations went up on the light post in town, the days were noticeably shorter, and anticipation would build as the tree went up in the corner of the living room. Presents began to appear under the tree. It was a short period but it produced the most excitement over a short period…the waiting season …Christmas.

The Waiting Season can arrive any time of year, for Kenna and I it was September, all three times. It arrived by way of a kit from the drug store and was later confirmed by the doctor, the news…nine months and we would be bringing home our baby… the *waiting season*. This is one season that commercialism has been unable to lengthen and science has been unable to shorten, it has remained nine months for most. The joy, the excitement, the anticipation, there is no way to describe it. Strange things happen during this time. It's not all cookies and cream, no, it might be apple juice and peanut butter, or watermelon and punch at midnight…yum. The instant your brain finds out, something happens to the bladder to both mother and father. The carpet gets worn out between the bedroom and bathroom.

Bad news! (Or good news.) Things never return to normal… Children!

It arrived the first week in October by way of an e-mail, my cell phone had gone dead, thus begins this *waiting season.* This *waiting season* is not one of great joy, or excitement. In this world all things are not exciting or enjoyable. How can this be, just this morning I had told a friend how thankful I was to have three healthy children and now the waiting season has began. This wait has sparked disbelief, anxiety, helplessness, where has my faith gone, where is my trust. I had faith, I had trust when it was me but now it's my youngest child. I keep telling myself that it's nothing and why am I fearing the worst. The message was that her test came back abnormal. The doctor said to come back in next Monday. A short week that already seems like an eternity. Thus the *waiting season…* a time for prayer, renewed faith and trust. New test, with all the world's technology you would think these tests results would be immediate….next week we will know…waiting season, Cancer?... No!... All clear!

Chapter 28
Master Cotton Chopper

Okay so with some slight of hand it helped Ehud free the Israelites from King Eglon in the Old Testament. Personally, I have found it to be of no advantage and usually it is a hindrance. Being left-handed has never been a walk in the park. The world caters to the majority and right-handed is the majority. Everything is made for the right-handed person thus making learning a new skill, with some tool, that much harder. Mrs. Denton tried, Mrs. Midge tried, Mrs. Betty tried, but if this were handwritten there would be one person that could read it…me. You should have pity on someone with such poor handwriting. I tried slanting that pencil and paper to the left, I tried it to the right, even tried upside down…nothing worked. Then we had to start using notebooks that either had this spiral wire or three big rings right where the left hand rests to write. I admire people who have good penmanship. Because of computers, penmanship is reported to be getting worse among our youth and not just the lefties.

Another tool that I can't use very well is the paintbrush, and it has nothing to do with being left-handed. I despise, absolutely hate, to paint and now that I am older and somewhat in control of what I have to do, I refuse to paint. It takes me twice as long and twice as much paint as it would the professional. The extra paint is on surfaces on which the paint does not belong, and the extra time is spent removing the paint from that surface. I just never could master the paint brush. Having failed at mastering painting makes watching people who can paint…the pros, even more astounding. No lost effort, every drop of paint where it should go, and when they are done, surprise…it looks good!

Going through one of those home improvement department stores I came to the "garden tools" section. I enjoy browsing this section, don't know why, I don't have a garden. I can't say that the urge to till the ground, prepare the soil, plant seed, and tend to it's productivity hasn't hit me before, It has…ONCE…. two rows of corn, two rows of green beans, six squash plants, five tomato plants, six banana pepper plants and finally, two hot pepper plants took care of that urge once and for all (see feelings about painting above).

Footnotes: Don't plant hot peppers next to sweet peppers, those little bees get confused on which pepper plant to leave pollen. Also when dehydrating chili peppers… do it outside!

More on that in the story: *So You Had To Leave Your House for a Week*. We'll leave that for another time!

This store had all the garden tools one could imagine. Today most of the adults that were around when I was growing up would find this section amusing. The heading "Garden Section" brings with it a connotation of enjoyment, recreation, hobby, or flowers. I don't think that was the case with them. It was a matter of having enough food to feed the family for the entire year. Many of the tools found in this section are tools for making a living, actually job related. Using this tool meant they would get paid at the end of the day, it is a way of life.

At the garden section I was reminded of another skill I never mastered…chopping cotton. A method of removing grass and weeds from the crop that was being grown using a hoe, which is basically about a four inch square blade at the end of a five foot handle. I never understood why it was called chopping cotton when it's the weeds you are chopping. Same as the pencil and paint brush…I used the wrong technique. Raising the hoe high above your head and forcefully chopping down on the plant was bad. My technique could be described as "cotton hacking." The idea being that you take the grass and leave the cotton. But the weeds and grass grew right next to the cotton. My technique causes one to remove the grass AND some of the cotton plants, causing the owner to frown, it also lends itself to the possible removal of one or more of the users own toes, causing a frown upon the amputees face.

Put a hoe in the hands of a master and it is something to behold. First of all, the master had their own hoe that only they were allowed to touch. This hoe had character. It had a handle that was worn where the user had placed their hands over and over through the years not just a day or two. They were wooden handles, not the fiberglass "improvements" of today's tools. The hoe's blade was worn down from years of use and being sharpened. And talk about sharp, some of those men could sharpen a hoe so sharp one could shave the hair on his arm, and they would gladly show you that it would do so. We part timers had to pick a hoe out of a stack of hoes that was used by whomever happened to be working that day. They were not as useful not having been in the master's hand for numerous years. The technique used by the skilled choppers was one of a very short, almost effortless "scrape". They could walk, carry on a conversation, chop two rows, and carefully remove the grass that was growing right next to the cotton leaving the cotton unharmed.

Romans 6:13 says we are to be instruments of righteous. We can only do this in the hands of the master. As instruments, can people see where the master has had his hands on us, not just part time but day after day? Do we allow the master to sharpen us to make us more useful? We are not talking about the tools of the recreational gardener, these tools placed in the master's hands is a matter of life eternal.

I found out that not only could my Mom walk, carry on a conversation, and hoe two rows, she could reach over with the hoe handle a raise a knot on a youngster's head who was not paying attention to what he was doing.

Such was the life of one of the Johnson kids, growing up in northeast Arkansas. Amen and pass the biscuits!